Hinduism
and
Mental Health

Harold G. Koenig, M.D.

DEDICATION

To my Father

CONTENTS

Introduction 1

1 Sacred Hindu Texts 3

2 Hindu Beliefs and Practices 10

3 Brahman 16

4 Hinduism Today 22

5 Hinduism and Mental Health: Speculations 31

6 Early Research 37

7 Latest Research 51

8 Research Summary and Future Directions 72

9 Applications in Clinical Practice 77

10 Conclusions 83

References 85

About the Author 100

ACKNOWLEDGMENTS

Madhu Sharma for her expertise in Hinduism

INTRODUCTION

In the third millennium BCE, a nomadic tribal people called the Aryas moved south from ancient Iran (some say southern Russia by the Caspian Sea) and settled in the Indus Valley, which extends from present day northeast Afghanistan to Pakistan and northwest India. They brought with them an early Sanskrit language and orally-transmitted religious beliefs and scriptures (Rg Veda) that would later evolve and expand into what was to become the third largest religion in the world. The Aryas (or Indo-Aryans) worshiped many different gods and goddesses, and used fire in their rituals and sacrifices. They organized themselves into the Indus Valley Civilization (2600–1600 BCE), one of the three earliest civilizations (along with Egyptian and Mesopotamian). The word "Hindu" to describe this religion was popularized in the late 19th century by the book *Hinduism*, written by the Oxford scholar Sir Monier Monier-Williams (1877).

By 2010 there were 1.03 billion Hindus (15% of the world's population), second in number only to Christians and Muslims (Pew Research Center, 2015). By 2050 the number of Hindus is projected to reach 1.38 billion based on current birthrates (2.4 births per woman). Most Hindus (94%) now live in India. In addition to India, Hinduism is the most common religion of Nepal, Mauritius in East Africa, and Bali in Indonesia. In the United States (U.S.), Hindus made up 0.6% of the population in 2010 (1.9 million) and are expected to double that percentage to 1.2% by 2050 (4.7 million). In Europe, Hindus currently make up 0.2% of Europe's population (1.4 million), but are also expected to double that percentage to 0.4% (2.7 million) by 2050 due mainly to immigration. With regard to age, 30% of Hindus were under age 15 in 2010 and 62% were between age 15 and 60 years, making it second only to Islam in terms of youth.

In this small book, I first describe the sacred texts on which Hinduism is based. I then concisely describe the beliefs and practices of Hindus, and examine exactly what Hindus believe and practice today (based on original data collected from three national and cross-national datasets). Based on these Hindu beliefs and practices, I speculate on the relationship between religiosity and mental health, hypothesizing both positive and negative effects. To put these speculation to the test, I conduct a review of quantitative research on

1

religiosity and mental health in Hindus (along with a comparison of mental health in Hindus and non-Hindus). Both early research published prior to 2010 (based on a systematic review) is presented and the most recent research published during the past decade is described. As part of the latter, I present information based on an original analysis of worldwide datasets comparing the well-being of Hindus and non-Hindus and examining the relationship between religiosity and well-being in Hindus. Finally, I make suggestions for mental health professionals on how to apply this knowledge about Hindu belief and practice and the findings from research when treating Hindu clients.

The **primary audience** for this book is mental health professionals and clergy who are called upon to help Hindus deal with emotional and other mental health problems. However, given the careful attention to documentation, emphasis on research, and report of original research results, investigators who conduct studies in Hindu populations, as well as healthcare systems that provide services to Hindu clients, will also find this volume useful. Finally, lay Hindus more generally will discover that the information contained here may be both enlightening and faith enhancing.

CHAPTER 1

SACRED HINDU TEXTS

The original scriptures of the Hindus are the Vedas, Upanishads, and the great Epics of Ramayana and Mahabharata (from which the Bhagavad Gita comes). In order to understand Hinduism, it is essential to know something about these texts written in the ancient language of Sanskrit.

Vedas
The earliest sacred scriptures on which Hinduism is based are the Vedas, which consist of four texts: the Rigveda (or Rg Veda), the Yajurveda, the Samaveda, and the Atharvaveda (**Figure 1**). The oldest Vedic text, the Rigveda (and the other Vedic texts as well) consists of verses (*samhita*), hymns, forest books (*aranyakas*)and ritual manuals (*brahmanas*) with chants, incantations, and mantras that were involved in an early sacrificial religious system dating back to 1700-1100 BCE (Narayana, 2016; Olivelle, 2016). From its very origins, the Vedic religion involved the offering of sacrifices to various Vedic gods (Indra, Varuna, Surya, etc.), and ceremonies which became more and more complex as the centuries passed requiring an expansion of the Vedic collections. The sacrifices, performed by the

brahmins (Vedic priests), were thought to produce rewards in this life and the next life (including the maintenance of ancestors in the afterlife). The later Vedas and especially the Upanishads described the meaning of the sacrifices and "secret" interpretation of how the sacrifices performed at the local or micro level allowed the emergence of favorable events in the physical universe on the macro level (Williams et al., 2012, p 7). These sacrifices, in fact, were believed to keep the entire cosmos running.[1]

According to Professor Gavin Flood (2009a) from Oxford Centre for Hindu studies in the United Kingdom, the four Vedas were written down in Sanskrit some time during the Vedic Period between 1500 and 500 BCE, although were passed down orally long before that. As noted in the Introduction, the content of these texts originated with the Aryas moving into the Indus Valley, whose civilization was fully developed by about 2,500 BCE. However, the origins of these texts may have been in the Neolithic period (10,000-4,500 BCE) when humans first began raising crops and keeping livestock rather than relying on hunting (requiring social harmony and group cooperation). The concept of *dharma* is first mentioned in the Rigveda, where it has been variously translated as "law," "duty," "order," "model," and "good works," and is repeated multiple times in later Hindu texts (see below). Dharma has to do with right action and involves moral and religious laws, and so is integral to the Hindu belief system today.

Upanishads
The Upanishads are commentaries on the Vedas and include some of the last portions of the Vedas themselves (called the *vendanta*, i.e., "conclusion of the Vedas"). They are made up of a series of over 200 surviving texts composed in Sanskrit prose or verse between 800 BCE and 100 BCE, of which 14 texts are primary: Brihadaranyaka, Chandogya, Taittiriya, Aitareya, Kaushitaki, Kena, Katha, Isa, Svetasvatara, Mundaka, Prasna, Mandukya, Mahanarayana, and

---

[1] As an aside, it is interesting to note that "sacrifice" also played a crucial role in the origins of Judaism (with the act of Abraham sacrificing his son Isaac and other sacrifices described in the Torah, including the passover) and Christianity (the sacrifice of Jesus on the cross as the sacrificial lamb). This continues today in the beliefs and practices of these faith traditions, as it does among present day Hindus (who offer small sacrifices in household shrines, see next chapter).

Maitri. The Upanishads include stories to illustrate the Vedic philosophy, rites and rituals, and are foundational theological texts on which many Hindu traditions are based. They were likely written by numerous different Indian sages at different time periods. The word Upanishad (spelled Upanisad in Sanskrit), which translated literally means "at the foot/feet sitting down" (u pa nishat), refers to the student sitting at the feet of the master, receiving secret knowledge.

Upanishad also means "connection," and the Upanishad texts focus primarily on the connection between the core of the individual person (*atman* or spiritual Self, soul, or Personal Essence) and celestial entities or forces, emphasizing the inter-connectedness of everything in the universe (Olivelle, 1996; 2016). In the Upanishads, the term *Brahman* is used to describe that eternal, conscious, irreducible, infinite, omnipresent, unchanging, and spiritual core of all that exists (the Universal Essence). This understanding of Brahman reflects the pantheistic view of God in Hinduism, the belief that God is in and about everything, and that the Personal Essence *is* the Universal Essence (Williams et al, 2012, p 7). Emphasis on looking inward and personal experience, then, became primary.

The Upanishads (specifically, the Aitareya and Chandogya) emphasize four stages of life or ashramas. Stage 1 (ages 0-25 years) focuses on training and learning, especially the learning of a profession or trade. This is called the *Bramacharya* or student stage. Stage 2 (ages 25-50) is the time for raising a family and engaging in work. This is called the *Grihastha* or householder stage. Stage 3 (ages 50-75) is when a person begins to detach from this life and focus on the spiritual life to come. This is called the *Vanaprastha* or retired stage. Stage 4 (ages 75-100) is where a person is nearing or becomes detached from life (often as a monk) and prepares for death and reincarnation. This is called the *Sannyasa* or renunciation stage (the earliest Upanishads combined the 3rd and 4th stages into one.

Villagers or "householders" spent most of their lives in the first two stages and were distinguished from the brahmins or priestly class, who performed rituals and interpreted the Vedas. There was another group in the 6th and 5th centuries BCE, however, who chose early in life to renounce the world and to wander about seeking the truth (rather than wait for the third/fourth stage in old age). Some of these renouncers were to reject the Hindu rituals, ceremonies, and gods, setting the stage for the emergence of Buddhism.

Figure 1. Historical timeline for Hinduism

Indus Valley Civilization
(2,600-1,600 BCE)

Vedas
(Rigveda, Yajurveda, Samaveda, Atharvaveda)
(1,700-900 BCE)

Upanishads
(14 known Upanishads)
(600-100 BCE)

Renouncers, Wanderers, Seekers[1]
600-500 BCE

Epic Period
(Ramayana and Mahabharata)
(400-100 BCE)

Bhagavad Gita
(based on the Mahabharata)
(300-200 BCE)

Rise of Devotional Hinduism
(300-1,000 CE)

Worship in Temples
(500-700 CE)

Residents of India begin to refer to themselves as "Hindus"
(1500-1600 CE)

Hinduism as a religion is popularized
(1877 CE)

Sources: Narayanan, 2016; Olivelle, 2016; Doniger, 2015; Williams et al., 2001)

---

[1] Buddhism begins as an offshoot of Hinduism

Ramayana and Mahabharata Epics

The Ramayana is an epic poem (composed around 400-300 BCE) that describes the reincarnation of Brahman (Vishnu) as a human named Rama. Rama was a good person who came to defeat and kill Revana, a demon king who kidnaps Rama's wife and is the primary antagonist in this poem.

The Mahabharata (composed somewhat later than the Ramayana) is the longest of the epic poems and is about the struggle for sovereignty between two groups of cousins, the Kauravas and the Pandavas. The Mahabharata is considered to be a text about *dharma*, which as described above involves the laws of conduct for kings, warriors, and anyone seeking to attain freedom from continual rebirth into nirvana (oneness with Brahman). Brahman is reincarnated as Lord Krishna, and acts in a similar role as Rama in the Ramayana. A popular belief in Hinduism is that when the world becomes bad, Brahman (God) is born into the world as a human people like Rama or Lord Krishna, who comes to guide and protect the community.

Bhagavad Gita (or simply "Gita")

The Bhagavad Gita ("Song of God") is a part of the Mahabharata epic poem (chapters 23 to 40 of Book VI) and is based on the Vedas and Upanishads. It was thought to have been added to or expanded out of the Mahabharata in around the 3rd century BCE. However, the Gita was not actually written down in Sanskrit until around 100-200 CE (Doniger, 2015). Some Hindu traditionalists claim it existed as early as the 4th millennium BCE. Indeed, although considered part of the Mahabharata, the Gita is quite different from the rest of the epic and may have originated from elsewhere. It was translated from Sanskrit into English around 1795 by Sir Charles Wilkins (Violatti, 2013). The Gita is a relatively brief volume containing approximately 700 verses in 18 short chapters, making it much more assessable to a general audience than other primary Hindu texts.

Because of its brevity and accessibility, the Bhagavad Gita is the most widely known and loved of all Hindu sacred scriptures. While the Vedas are considered the philosophical and ritualistic parts of Hinduism, the Gita is considered the heart of this faith tradition, containing religious aspects that make up its core. Indeed, the Gita not only addresses the topic of how to live, the duty to self, and the duty to community, but also describes key characteristics of Brahman or God as viewed by Hindus (see below). Mahatma Gandhi, Ralph Waldo Emerson, and Henry David Thoreau are said to have used the Bhagavad Gita as a primary reference, and the British in India during the 19th century claimed it was the Hindu equivalent of the New Testament (Doniger, 2015). The focus of the text has been described as "the search for serenity, calmness, and permanence in a world of rapid change and how to integrate spiritual values into ordinary life" (Violatti, 2013). Translator W.J. Johnson (1994, p i) calls it "the most widely read Hindu religious text in the Western world."

The historical setting of the Bhagavad Gita is important to note. The Gita emerged at a time in history when Hinduism was being challenged and divided into splinter groups. These new religious groups (Jains and Buddhists) were pushing for an ascetic lifestyle that emphasized the withdrawal from society, including withdrawal from family, possessions, and occupation (renouncers, wanderers, truth-seekers, as noted above). The Gita, however, argues that one can engage in a spiritual life based on actions in the world (*dharma*) without withdrawing from the world (i.e., entering into eternal existence or *sanatana*). Just as in Christianity, then, there is a tension between "works" and "faith."

With regard to the Bhagavad Gita's content, this sacred scripture involves a conversation between Lord Krishna and Arjuna. Lord Krishna is considered (like Rama before him) to be an *avatar* or incarnation of Brahman (Vishnu), the One Supreme God. Arjuna was a great archer and member of the warrior class (*Kshatriyas*). His duty was to lead the Pandavas into battle against the Kauravas (warring cousins, see Mahabharata epic above). Lord Krishna comes into the world in the form of Arjuna's charioteer / body guard / court historian. Before the battle begins, Arjuna realizes that the fight will involve killing his relatives, teachers, and friends (the Kauravas), and so rather than kill those he loves and thereby incur bad karma, he throws down his arrows and quits. His charioteer Lord Krishna consoles and advises him, emphasizing that it is his duty as a warrior to engage in battle. Out of this conversation come many of the basic tenets of Hinduism.

Conclusions

The most sacred Hindu texts are the Vedas, Upanishads, and the great Epics of Ramayana and Mahabharata. The earliest scriptures on which Hinduism is based are the four Veda texts, the Rigveda, the Yajurveda, the Samaveda, and the Atharvaveda. The earliest of these (the Rigveda) were written down over 3000 years ago at some time during the second millennium before the common era (BCE), and likely transmitted orally long before that. The Vedas primarily consist of hymns, chants, and incantations involved in the offering of sacrifices. Sacrifices were at first made to Indira, the god of the sacrificial fire or Surya, the sun god). The gods were expected to reciprocate by providing prosperity to those for whom the sacrifices were being offered. The Upanishads are commentaries on the Vedas that illustrate the Vedic philosophy and theology. Based on the Vedas and the Upanishads, the most recent Hindu scripture is the Bhagavad Gita that emerged from the Mahabharata epic in the second or third century BCE, but was not written down until the second or third century CE. The Bhagavad Gita is the most widely read and loved of all the Hindu scriptures.

CHAPTER 2

HINDU BELIEFS AND PRACTICES

There is great diversity in religious belief and practice among Hindus. Rooted in the original Hindu texts above, these have emerged and changed over time and geographic location. They have been shaped and formed by a variety of Hindu sages and scholars, resulting in a vast array of spiritual material (and different philosophical schools). The present goal is to identify and describe the basic Hindu beliefs common to a majority of these diverse traditions. According to the *Encyclopedia Britannica*, there are five elements that form the bedrock of the Hindu religion (Narayanan, 2016). These elements are doctrine, practice, society, story, and devotion.

Doctrine
Hindu beliefs revolve around three major concepts: *dharma* (world-preserving action, based on moral and religious laws); *moksha* (non-attachment, release and withdrawal from the materialistic world, which is flawed); and *karma* (the effect of one's actions on present and future reincarnated lives).

As noted in Chapter 1, dharma (world-preserving action) and moksha (withdrawal from the world) are in constant tension, which the Bhagavad Gita seeks to balance. The Gita stresses five principles, which have their origins in the Vedas and Upanishads:

(1) *SaguNa Brahman*. This refers to the personal characteristics of the Universal Essence or Supreme God (also sometimes referred to as *Paratman*). These personal features stand in contrast to the impersonal or transcendent characteristics of God (*NriguNa Brahman*). Recall that Lord Krishna (the incarnation of the Supreme God) appears in the Gita as a person.

(2) *Jiva*. This is the "true Self" of the individual human (*atman*) and is distinguished from the false self or ego. The atman is part of the Paratman just like water molecules in an ocean wave are part of the ocean.

(3) *Prakriti*. This refers to material nature, which is temporary and under the control of the Supreme God (and part of the Supreme God). The material nature consists of three modes or "Gunas": (1) goodness, light, or harmony; (2) energy, activity or passion; and (3) inertia, darkness or ignorance.

(4) *Kala* (time). All persons and things are under the influence of eternal time, where material existence is created, maintained, and then destroyed at regular intervals in an endless cycle. Lord Krishna says "I am time run on, destroyer of the universe, risen here to annihilate worlds" (11:32[1]).

(5) *Karma* (activity). All actions in this world cause re-actions. Humans have free will, and their destiny is in their own hands (as in the Christian tradition, "as you sow, so shall you reap").

With regard to karma, Hindus believe that the present life is not the end. When leaving this life at death, one is reincarnated and begins the next life. Those living a good life will be reborn into a good family (or higher caste, see below). Those not living a good life will be reborn into a lower caste with a more difficult life.

The doctrine of re-birth cannot be found in the earliest Vedas, and it is not clear where this belief emerged from (Williams et al, 2012, p 8). However, with the belief in rebirth (reincarnation) came

---

[1] All quotations from the Bhagavad Gita are taken from W.J. Johnson (1994). *The Bhagavad Gita* (Oxford World's Classics). NY, NY: Oxford University Press

the reality of re-death, which Vedic thinkers struggled with, since the prospect of dying over and over again for eternity was disturbing. Thus came the belief that this endless series of rebirths (*samsara*) and re-deaths would continue <u>until</u> the person realized the connection between their true self (atman) and the rest of reality and thereby merge with Paratman (God) and become free from the cycle of rebirth after death (*moksha*).

Lord Krishna in the Gita described three ways to accumulate good karma and avoid bad karma that perpetuated *samsara*, and therefore ensure a good rebirth and ultimately achieve *moksha*:

(1) way of knowledge (realizing that life and death are not real but an illusion, which is a view based on the Vedas and Upanishads)
(2) way of action or dharma (to act in good, heroic, or brave ways without concern for the outcome)
(3) way of devotion (surrendering the will to Lord Krishna, who will himself take on the bad karma)

These three ways to accumulate good karma have helped to form the different castes in India, although are not limited to any one particular caste. The *way of knowledge* was originally meant for the highest brahmin caste (teachers, priests, those who organized and studied the Vedas). The *way of action* was intended for the middle warrior caste, emphasizing that emotions such as fear or anxiety interfered with the outcomes being sought (such as victory during wartime). This came to mean more generally that selfish attachments to things or people should be avoided so as not to become elated over good fortune or depressed over misfortune. Lord Krishna emphasized that attachments (longings for people, possessions, or other non-permanent things) bring sorrow, fear, and anger. These emotions result in loss of understanding, which leads to perishing. Finally, the *way of devotion* was meant for the lower peasant or common people's caste, emphasizing the relationship to Lord Krishna himself. For most of society, then, love and worship of God – which involved surrender to the divine will -- was the surest way to accumulate good karma and ultimately merge with God.

Practice

Hindus focus on ritual and cultural practices, family-oriented rites of passage, annual festivals, and pilgrimages, spending less attention on specific doctrines like those described above. Vedic rituals and worship often involve icons or images (representing various aspects of the Supreme God, Brahman). Hindus do not worship millions of gods (as some critics claim), but rather worship many deities who are believed to be manifestations of the one supreme God (Basu, 2017). *Puja* (meaning "honoring or showing reverence for the deity") involves invocations, prayers, songs, and rituals. These rituals may include the offering and sharing of food (in earlier Vedic times called "sacrifices") as one might do for a guest to show honor for that person. Worship involves expressions of gratitude to the deity for allowing them to be born into this world and dependence on the deity for everything. Rituals reflect the belief that all persons are equal before God and part of God (despite being of different castes or classes in society). Hindus worship in temples, which may be buildings located in the community or small shrines located in private homes. The Hindu priest is a clergy person trained to perform services or sacrifices at a temple. The priest is different than a "guru," who is a Hindu teacher or wise man (not necessarily a priest).

Meditation may be performed in order to focus the mind on a single object, word or sound that represents the inner spiritual Self (atman) as part of God (Paratman). Yoga is a practice that combines meditation and physical postures, and originated in the ascetic practices of ancient India. Yoga (and the practitioner called a "yogin") is mentioned in the earliest of the Upanishads, the Brihadaranyaka (1:5:23) and in the Bhagavad Gita (6:1-4). Yoga (meaning in Sanskrit "to unite" mind and body) has evolved over time into a group of mental, physical, and spiritual disciplines, with the best known forms today being Hatha and Raja yoga. Systematic research indicates that 8.9% of adults in the U.S. report they practiced yoga at least once during the past 12 months (Cramer et al., 2016). However, the Westernized form of yoga that emphasizes exercise, postures, and breathing techniques is quite different from the yoga practiced in India (Adler, 2012).

The practice of yoga by Hindus in India is actually not very frequent, at least according to anecdotal reports (Roy, 2010). In one of the few epidemiologic studies of yoga from India, researchers found that only 4% of Indian adults (43 of 904) practiced yoga (Nayak et al., 2011). The most common form of stress relaxation practiced by Hindus in that study was "religious activity," which far surpassed yoga in prevalence. One report of patients with schizophrenia in India found that among those who were eligible to participate in a clinical trial involving yoga, more than half (56.8%) declined to participate; although logistical factors were primary in preventing participation, other reasons for refusal included not being willing to practice yoga, religious reasons for not participating, and other personal reasons (Baspure et al., 2012). Thus, while the origins of yoga are in the Hindu scriptures, the practice is surprisingly not very common among Hindus in India.

Transcendental Meditation (TM) is a form of meditation developed by Maharishi Mahesh Yogi (known as "the guru to the Beatles") in the mid-1900s. TM has its origin in the Advaita Vendata school of Hindu philosophy and religious practice. The prevalence of TM among Hindus in India is unknown, but not likely high since TM is largely a Western meditative practice.

Society

Society in early India was organized into four classes called *castes*, a practice that to some extent still exists today. The castes are based on four parts of the human body described in a Vedic hymn that serve as a model for the structure of community (Rigveda 10:90). Those castes are *brahmins* (or priests and teachers who, as noted above, traditionally read, taught, and interpreted the Vedas), *kshatriyas* (warriors or nobles), *vaishyas* (peasants or common people), and *shudras* (servants or slaves). A person's caste is determined by the family that he or she is born into, and that person is expected to follow the same occupational profession as other members of the family/caste. All four castes, at least in theory, are to be respected equally, although represent different levels of "purity," with brahmins representing the most pure, which was necessary since they performed the sacrifices (at least in early Vedic times).

Story

Stories of interactions between humans and divine beings have for millennia held the Hindu community together, provided role models, and given meaning to daily events and relationships. These narratives include the stories of Rama and his wife, Sita; Lord Krishna and his female companion, Radha; Shiva and his lover, Parvati; and Devi, known as the demon-slayer. In these stories, God enters into the world as a human being and interacts with others to combat evil and promote good, endorse right behavior, and address social problems. These stories teach how one should live based on the principles of dharma.

Devotion

This aspect of Hinduism has the most overlap with Western religious traditions such as Christianity, and Catholicism in particular. B*hakti* ("devotion" or "attachment") is the word given to loving and worshiping God as manifested by various Hindu deities or by Indian poets or saints. Practicing devotion to these manifestations of God is a big part of Hindu life. The writings of Indian poets and saints have been critical to the evolution of the caste system, image worship, religious vows, pilgrimages, and acts of self-discipline or denial.

Conclusions

The Hindu religion involves the elements of doctrine, practice, society, story, and devotion. Hindu beliefs focus on *dharma* (world-preserving actions based on moral and religious laws), *moksha* (non-attachment to the materialistic world), and *karma* (the direct effect of one's actions on present and future reincarnated lives). Hindu practices involve rituals, meditations, family-oriented rites of passage, festivals, and pilgrimages. Vedic rituals and worship often involve icons or images that represent various aspects of the Supreme God, Brahman. Society was organized in the past and to some extent even today around the four basic castes (priests/teachers, warriors/nobles, common people, and servants/slaves). Stories involving Rama, Lord Krishna, Shiva, and Devi provide role models and give meaning to daily events and relationships. Finally, devotion involves loving and worshiping the Supreme God in God's many manifested forms through the worship of various Hindu deities, Indian poets and saints. This leads to a fuller discussion in the next chapter of what the term "God" means in Hinduism.

CHAPTER 3

BRAHMAN

Because of the central place that Brahman plays in Hindu belief and worship, and the potential overlap with the western notion of God, a more detailed examination of this central deity in Hinduism is warranted. There were many other gods or devas during the Vedic period including *earth* gods (plant god Soma, fire god Agni, and priestly power god Brhaspati), *atmosphere* gods (warrior god Indra, wind god Vayu, storm god Maruts, and the capricious god Rudra, who had both good and bad qualities), and *sky* gods (sky god Dyaus, cosmic law god Varuna, night god Mitra, and nourisher god Pushan) (Flood, 2009a). Brahman was first mentioned in the Taittiriya Samhita VII.3.1.4 (one of the oldest Vedic texts), and subsequently became prominent in hundreds of later Vedic hymns. The word Brahman in Sanskrit means "the Supreme God," "the Absolute Reality," or "Godhead." Further descriptions are contained in the Upanishads. The Mundaka Upanishad describes Brahman as:

"Brahman alone here extends to the east; Brahman, to the west; it alone, to the south, to the north, it alone extends above and below; it is Brahman alone that extends over this whole universe, up to its widest extent" (2:2:11)[1].

---

[1] All Upanishad quotes cited here are from: Olivelle P (1996). *Upanishads* (Oxford World Classics). Oxford, UK: Oxford University Press

Brahman is the one eternal cause and foundation of all existence, the transcendent power that exists beyond the universe and supports everything, the Ultimate Reality.

According to Flood (1996), the concept of Brahman evolved during the Vedic period from (a) the power contained in sound (specifically, the syllable *Om*), words, and rituals, and (b) the "essence of the universe"... the "deeper foundation of all phenomena"... the "essence of the self (Atman, soul)"...and the "truth of a person beyond apparent difference." Brahman has many characteristics similar to Western notions of God, but is not exactly equivalent to God, says Flood. However, Hindus in actual practice have many different beliefs and they do not always agree on those beliefs, making it difficult to make any definitive statements about similarities and differences between Brahman and the notion of God in the West.

Hindus do not worship Brahman as Jews, Christians or Muslims worship God. However, they may worship manifestations of Brahman such as Vishnu and Shiva (BBC 2003). Brahman is manifested in three forms as a trinity (or *Trimurti*): Brahma (the creator), Vishnu (the preserver), and Shiva (the transformer). Brahma (different from Brahman) created the universe, and so his work is done and he is not worshiped. Vishnu preserves the universe, whereas Shiva destroys the universe, and both may be worshiped as manifestations of Brahman.

Vishnu (also called Vasudeva, Narayana, or Hari) was not a major god during the Vedic period, and was worshiped as the Sun god (Doniger, 2015). This changed over time, such that Hindus now worship Vishnu as a manifestation of Brahman. Vishnu preserves and protects the universe and has appeared on the earth through his incarnations as Rama, Lord Krishna and Narasimha. During the Gupta Empire (320-500 CE), the great traditions of Vaishnavism (focused on Vishnu), Shaivism (focused on Shiva), and Shaktism (focused on Devi, a female manifestation of Brahman) developed. It is from this period that many elements of Hinduism arose such as bhakti (devotion) and worship in temples (Flood, 2009a).

Closely related to the concept of Brahman is atman. As noted above, atman is the "spiritual Self" beyond the ego or the "false self," and is considered the eternal spirit or soul that each human possesses. The word atman itself means "eternal self," which is in contrast to the temporary body. The atman can exist in more than one body across time, as the essence of the individual is reborn during the process of reincarnation. The atman is God within the person, representing their true identity. In the Brhadaranyaka Upsanishad it says:

"If a man knows 'I am *brahman*' in this way, he becomes this whole world. Not even the gods are able to prevent it, for he becomes their very self (*atman*). So when a man venerates another deity, thinking, 'He is one, and I am another', he does not understand…It is his self (atman) alone that a man should venerate as his world. And if someone venerates his self alone as his world, that rite of his will never fade away, because from his very self he will produce whatever he desires." (1:4:10, 15)

This concept of the true Self (spirit or soul) as non-material has encouraged detachment from the world and promoted asceticism in Hinduism (Flood, 2009b).

Personal God
As noted above, the understanding of "Brahman" evolved and expanded over time in ancient India, and there is now a range of views concerning the nature of Brahman (Flood, 1996). As noted above, many Hindus believe that Brahman does not have attributes or form (N*rigu*N*a Brahman* or "the Highest Absolute") and so is beyond all description and conceptualization:

"What cannot be seen, what cannot be grasped, without color, without sight or hearing, without hands or feet; What is eternal and all-pervading, extremely minute, present everywhere -- What is the immutable, which the wise fully perceive" (Mundaka Upanishad 1:1:6).

However, there is also belief that Brahman may take a personal form that has good attributes (*SaguNa Brahman* or "the Absolute with qualities") (see discussion by Stephen Knapp, 2016). The notion that there is a personal aspect to Brahman that is loving, gives grace, and can be the subject of devotion and worship (bhakti) comes from the Shvetashvatara Upanishad. Here it states:

"The one God rules over both the perishable and the self (atman). By meditating on him, by striving towards him, and, further, in the end by becoming the same reality as him, all delusion disappears. When one has known God, all the fetters fall off; by eradication of the blemishes, birth and death come to an end; by meditating on him, one obtains, at the dissolution of the body, a third—sovereignty over all; and in the absolute one's desires are fulfilled." (1:10-11)

Elsewhere the Svetasvatara Upanishad states:

"Who is higher than that, higher than Brahman, the immense one hidden in all beings, in each according to its kind, and who alone encompasses the whole universe -- when people know him as Lord, they become immortal. I know that immense Person, having the color of the sun and beyond darkness. Only when a man knows him does he pass beyond death; there is no other path for getting there. This whole world is filled by that Person, beyond whom there is nothing; beneath whom there is nothing; smaller than whom there is nothing; larger than whom there is nothing; and who stands like a tree planted firmly in heaven." (3:7-9)

This suggests a "pantheistic" notion of God as being in and part of everything. It was not until the Bhagavad Gita, though, that a "new dimension of love of God for people and people for God" was introduced, says professor Mariasusai Dhavamony[1] (2002, p 88). The characteristics of Lord Krishna (the eighth incarnation of Vishnu/ Brahman) provides clues about the personal nature of Brahman. In the Gita, as noted earlier, Lord Krishna engages in relationships with devout believers and saves them from the effects of their own karma (similar to "grace" in Christianity). Consider the following quote from the Bhagavad Gita:

"Even the evil-doer, if he shares in me with single-minded devotion, may be thought of as good, for he has fixed on what is right. He quickly conforms to the true law and obtains

---

[1] Mariasusai Dhavamony is Professor of History of Religions and Hinduism at Gregorian University in Rome, Italy

everlasting peace. You should realize, Son of Kunti [Arjuna], that no devotee of mine is lost." (9:30-31)

According to Dhavammony (2002, p 88), the Gita emphasizes that good action and right living (dharma) "paves the way to liberation, it is through God's grace alone that one attains the liberated state and enters into union with him in love and bliss." Note also the following passages from the Gita (Lord Krishna speaking) that focus on knowledge, action/behavior, and devotion to him as God:

"For knowledge is better than study, meditation is superior to knowledge, and abandonment of the fruit of actions is better than meditation, and after abandonment peace immediately follows.

Without hatred for any creature, friendly and compassionate, free from possessiveness and egoism, indifferent to pleasure and pain, enduring, contented, ever the self-controlled yogin, certain of purpose, his mind and intelligence concentrated on me, he who is devoted to me is dear to me.

He is dear to me who does not afflict the world and is not afflicted by it -- who is free from excitement, impatience, fear, and anxiety.

He is dear to me who, devoted to me, is disinterested, pure, able, non-partisan, unworried, and does not initiate any actions.

He is dear to me who, filled with devotion, is neither excited nor repelled by things, neither grieves nor gives way to longing, and who abandons both the auspicious and the inauspicious.

The man is dear to me who, filled with devotion, is the same with regard to enemies and friends, in honor and dishonor, the same in heat and cold, pleasure and suffering, who, freed from attachment, weighs blame and praise the same, who was silent, satisfied in all circumstances, homeless, and firm-minded.

And above all, those devotees are dear to me who, full of faith, with me as their highest object, attend to this immortal nectar of truth, which I have just delivered to you."
(12:12-20; see also 18:65)

Conclusions

In Hinduism, then, Brahman can be worshiped as either God who is formless or as God who is personal and has attributes, both of whom are understood as the same One Supreme God. In practice, many Hindus relate to the personal aspects of Brahman as one who has attributes such as strength, power, and goodness, and is worthy of worship.

CHAPTER 4

HINDUISM TODAY

How do the Hindu beliefs, practices, and teachings based on the original Vedic texts relate to what Hindus today believe and practice? Indeed, these are the Hindus that mental health professionals and clergy around the world are likely to counsel. Presented here are data from three cross-national and national surveys involving large random samples of adults that include an assessment of Hindu religious affiliation, religious beliefs, and practices: the International Social Survey Program-III (ISSP, 2008), World Values Survey (WVS 2005-2006), and the Global Attitudes Project (GAP, 2009) (**Tables 1-3**) (Koenig, 2017, unpublished report).

Belief in God

The International Social Survey Program-III (ISSP, 2008) asked a random sample of almost 60,000 adults from 40 countries about their religious beliefs and practices of (**Table 1**). The sample included 203 Hindus from various countries (India was not included in this survey). Surprisingly, Hindus (70% from South Africa) were significantly *more likely* than members of other religious groups (89% Christian) to says that "I know God really exists and I have no doubts about it" (73.1% vs. 50.4%, p<0.0001). Almost all Hindus in this sample said that "I believe in God now and I always have," again a higher percentage than other religious groups (93.0% vs. 78.4%, p<0.0001). Furthermore, Hindus were more likely to say that "There is a God who concerns Himself with every human being personally" compared to non-Hindus (84.1% vs. 56.1%, p<0.0001), more likely to say that "life is meaningful only because God exists" (55.1% vs. 38.9%, p<0.0001), and more likely to agree to the statement "I have my own way of connecting with God without churches or religious services" (84.4% vs. 56.1%, p<0.0001).

Other cross-national random surveys of Hindus (particularly those that have included Hindus from India) have reported similar results, though not as striking. The 2005-2006 World Values Survey (WVS) examined a random sample of over 80,000 adults from more than 80 countries, including 1,962 Hindus primarily from India (77%) and Trinidad/Tobago (12%) (**Table 2**). When asked to rate "How important is God in your life" on a 1 to 10 scale (1=not at all important, 10=very important), Hindus on average scored only slightly lower (7.9 vs. 8.5) than members of other religious groups (61% of whom were Christian). Overall, then, belief in God and importance of God in life is surprisingly similar in Hindus compared to members of other religious groups around the world (including Muslims and Christians), although this is perhaps slightly less so in India.

Religiosity in General
Many Hindus indicate that religion is very important to them. The 2008 ISSP survey of 203 Hindus described above found that 41.0% of the sample indicated they were very or extremely religious compared to 20.5% of members of other religious groups. In the 2009 Global Attitudes Project (GAP), which included a random sample of 5,769 adults from India, Great Britain, Indonesia, Pakistan, and Canada (1,856 of whom were Hindus, 97% from India), participants were asked about the importance of religion in their lives. Hindus were somewhat less likely than persons from other religious groups to say that religion was "very important" to them (73.9% vs. 79.4%, p<0.001) (**Table 3**). However, Hindus were more likely to engage in religious practices compared to non-Hindus. In this sample, non-Hindus were primarily Muslims (70.0%) and Christians

23

(24.5%). Finally, in the 2005-2006 WVS (**Table 2**), which also included Hindus primarily from India, there was no difference in the proportion of Hindus indicating that religion was "very important" in life compared to non-Hindus (57.4% vs. 57.1%); likewise, 80.2% of Hindus described themselves as a "religious person" compared to 79.9% of non-Hindus. Similarly, Hindus were just as likely as non-Hindus to believe that children should have religious faith instilled in them at home (45.2% vs. 47.9% of non-Hindus). Therefore, there appears to be little difference between Hindus and members of other religious groups with regard to self-rated importance of religion in life, and in places like South Africa, Hindus are considerably more likely to report that religion is important to them than are non-Hindus.

Other Religious Beliefs

As noted above, core beliefs in Hinduism involve *dharma* (world-preserving action, based on moral and religious laws), *moksha* (non-attachment to, release and withdrawal from the material world), and *karma* (the effect of one's actions on present and future lives). They also included beliefs about the reincarnation of souls, the world of ancestors and gods, the Supreme God whom Hindus call Brahman, and about the need to respect all religions. As noted above, many Hindus believe in God, including a personal God. What about other core Hindu beliefs? Unfortunately, national random surveys that include large numbers of Hindus and that ask about the details of religious belief are not readily available. However, the 2008 ISSP provides important details on Hindu beliefs in a relatively small sample of Hindus (n=203), largely those from South Africa (**Table 1**).

In that survey, 73.4% of Hindus said they believe in life after death (vs. 66.0% of non-Hindus); 76.4% believe in heaven (vs. 68.4% of non-Hindus); 60.0% believe in hell (vs. 54.9% of non-Hindus); 79.7% believe in religious miracles (vs. 64.9% of non-Hindus); 72.9% believe in reincarnation (vs. 36.6% of non-Hindus); 68.2% believe in Nirvana (vs. 23.8% of non-Hindus); and 63.3% believe in the supernatural power of ancestors (vs. 34.4% of non-Hindus). Furthermore, 63.1% of Hindus believe in respect for all religions (vs. 36.2% of non-Hindus, p<0.0001), and 79.1% have positive attitudes toward Christians (vs. 73.5% of non-Hindus), 74.4% toward Muslims (vs. 35.4% of non-Hindus), 77.5% toward Buddhists (vs. 39.2% of non-Hindus), 72.9% of Jews (vs. 36.1% of non-Hindus), and even 53.9% have positive attitudes towards atheists (vs. 29.9% of non-Hindus). Thus, at least among Hindus in South Africa, Great Britain, and countries outside of India, Hindus tend to be a religious people who believe in God and many core Hindu beliefs such as life after death, heaven and hell, reincarnation, Nirvana, miracles, and respect for all religions (including respect for those without religious belief), often more so than members of other religious groups.

Religious Practices

To what degree are Hindus involved in religious practices? As noted above, common religious practices include worshiping, praying, and conducting rituals and making offerings at Hindu temples in the community or at shrines in their homes, going on pilgrimages, and meditating. The 2008 ISSP found that Hindus attend religious services to a similar degree as non-Hindus (22.9% weekly or more often, vs. 25.5% for non-Hindus). In the 2009 GAP survey (97% of Hindus from India), they were slightly more likely than non-Hindus to attend religious services (34.5% weekly or more often vs. 33.5% for non-Hindus). Results were similar in the 2005-2005 WVS (the vast majority of Hindus being from India), where 42.6% reported they attended religious services weekly or more frequently (vs. 41.3% of non-Hindus).

Two out of three surveys found that prayer was more common among Hindus than in members of other religious groups. In the 2008 ISSP, 64.9% of Hindus prayed daily or several times per day (vs. 29.2% of non-Hindus). In the 2009 GAP survey, 81.5% of Hindus (primarily from India) said they prayed daily or several times per day (vs. 46.3% of non-Hindus). Only in the 2005-2006 WVS were "moments of prayer or meditation" similar in Hindus compared to non-Hindus (82.5% vs. 82.4%). The ISSP also found that Hindus were more likely to have a religious shrine, altar, or icon in their homes (88.7% vs. 53.9% of non-Hindus), and more likely to go on pilgrimage, i.e., visit religious holy places other than temples for religious services (64.9% vs. 38.6% of non-Hindus). Thus, Hindus are often engaged in religious practices of their faith, sometimes more than are members of other religious faiths.

Table 1. Comparison of beliefs, attitudes and practices between Hindus, other religious groups, and the non-affiliated: *International Social Survey Program 2008*

	Hindus % (N)/Mean (SD)	Non-Hindus % (N)/Mean (SD)	No Affiliation % (N)/Mean (SD)
Sample size	100.0 (203)	100.0 (46,463)	100.0 (12,559)
Religious Beliefs			
Confidence in R@ groups (high)	56.6 (111) ***[1]	38.2 (17,031)	8.1 (939)
Trust too much in science, not R (agree)	47.7 (95) ***	32.3 (14,099)	15.9 (1,881)
We must respect all religions (agree)	63.1 (128) ***	36.2 (16,412)	28.3 (3,380)
Accept different R to marry relative	36.4 (72) ns	35.7 (15,619)	40.3 (4,633)
Current belief about God			
I know God really exists, no doubts	73.1 (147) ***	50.4 (23,155)	8.7 (1,083)
I believe in God, with some doubts	12.4 (25)	19.1 (8.760)	7.5 (928)
Believe in higher power, not personal God	3.0 (6)	9.5 (4,352)	9.0 (1,108)
Sometimes believe in God, & sometimes not	7.5 (15)	11.2 (5,129)	20.0 (2,478)
Don't know if there is God & can't find out	2.5 (5)	6.0 (2,737)	19.2 (2,373)
I don't believe in God	1.5 (3)	3.9 (1,794)	35.7 (4,416)
Present and past belief in God			
I believe in God now & always have	93.0 (173) ***	78.4 (31,604)	19.2 (1,970)
I believe in God now, but didn't used to	2.2 (4)	8.5 (3,429)	5.2 (529)
Don't believe in God now, but used to	1.6 (3)	6.5 (2,632)	23.4 (2,395)
Don't believe in God now & never have	3.2 (6)	6.6 (2,652)	52.2 (5,347)
Believe in life after death? (definite/prob)	73.4 (141) ns	66.0 (27,735)	31.5 (3,569)
Believe in heaven? (definitely/probably)	76.4 (149) ns	68.4 (28,732)	21.1 (2,390)
Believe in hell? (definitely/probably)	60.0 (114) ns	54.9 (22,830)	16.5 (1,864)
Believe in R miracles? (definite/probably)	79.7 (153) ***	64.9 (27,548)	21.3 (2,437)
Believe in reincarnation? (definite/prob)	72.9 (140) ***	36.6 (14,807)	23.2 (2,603)
Believe in Nirvana? (definitely/probably)	68.2 (30) ***	23.8 (6,982)	14.8 (1,398)
Believe supernatural power of ancestor?	63.3 (119) ***	34.4 (13,814)	22.1 (2,459)
God concerned over humans personally?	84.1 (164) ***	60.9 (26,403)	15.6 (1,785)
Is life meaningful only because of God?	55.1 (109) ***	38.9 (17,130)	7.0 (830)
I have my own way to connect with God, other than going to church (yes)	84.4 (168) ***	56.1 (24,447)	35.6 (3,844)

International Social Survey Program-III (2008) surveyed a random sample of 59,063 citizens ages 15-90 from 40 countries (Australia, Austria, Belgium - Flanders, Chile, Croatia, Cyprus, Czech Republic, Denmark, Dominican Republic, Finland, France, Germany, Great Britain, Hungary, Ireland, Israel, Italy, Latvia, Mexico, Netherlands, New Zealand, Northern Ireland, Norway, Philippines, Poland, Portugal, Russia, Slovakia, Slovenia, Spain, South Africa, Sweden, Switzerland, Turkey, Ukraine, Uruguay, the United States of America, Venezuela). **Note that Hindus in this sample come primarily from South Africa (69.5%) and Great Britain (10.8%);** non-Hindus were more equally distributed across all countries. Interviews were conducted face-to-face, by telephone, and self-completed postal questionnaires. The data downloaded from Association of Religion Data Archives, www.TheARDA.com, collected by Dr. Max Haller & team, Institut für Soziologie, Universität Graz, Austria (accessed 11/7/16).

Table 1. Comparison of beliefs, attitudes, practices and demographics between Hindus, other religions, and non-affiliated: *International Social Survey Program 2008* (continued)

	Hindus % (N)/Mean (SD)	Non-Hindus % (N)/Mean (SD)	No Affiliation % (N)/Mean (SD)
Sample size	100.0 (203)	100.0 (46,463)	100.0 (12,559)
Religious Beliefs/Attitudes			
How would you describe yourself?			
Very or extremely religious	41.0 (82) ***	20.5 (9,314)	2.4 (295)
What are your views concerning religion?			
Basic truths present in many religions	82.3 (158) ***	67.6 (27,575)	56.3 (5,584)
Follow R@, and interest in spirit/sacred	30.9 (59) ns	32.9 (13,819)	3.1 (351)
Positive attitude towards Christians	79.1 (129) ns	73.5 (16,910)	39.5 (2,463)
Positive attitude towards Muslims	74.4 (122) ***	35.4 (7,547)	19.8 (1,200)
Positive attitude towards Hindus	94.0 (157) ***	33.2 (6,701)	26.1 (1,532)
Positive attitude towards Buddhists	77.5 (124) ***	39.2 (7,978)	38.1 (2,276)
Positive attitude towards Jews	72.9 (113) ***	36.1 (7,490)	25.1 (1,497)
Positive attitude towards atheists	53.9 (84) ***	29.9 (6,226)	39.5 (2,408)
Religious Practices			
Attended R services ($\geq$weekly) at 10-11	35.4 (69) **	48.0 (21,399)	21.6 (2,575)
Attend R services ($\geq$weekly) now	22.9 (46) ns	25.5 (11,698)	1.3 (157)
Pray daily or several/day now	64.9 (131) ***	29.2 (13,323)	6.0 (736)
Have a R shrine/altar/icon in home	88.7 (180) ***	53.9 (24,849)	16.8 (2,098)
Visiting R holy place other than church			
At least once or twice per year	64.9 (131) ***	38.6 (17,738)	9.8 (1,218)
Demographics			
R affiliations			
Buddhist	0	2.6 (1,224)	0
Christian	0	85.7 (38,944)	0
Jewish	0	2.4 (1,104)	0
Islam	0	4.8 (2,167)	0
Hinduism	100.0 (203)	0	0
Other Christian religions	0	2.9 (1,333)	0
Other Eastern religions	0	2.6 (1,165)	0
Other religions	0	1.2 (536)	0
No religion	0	0	99.9 (12,548)
Believe in God, but no religion	0	0	0.1 (11)
Age, years	42.8 (16.1) **	47.2 (17.4)	44.4 (16.4)***[2]
Education (at least some college)	26.7 (54) ns	29.5 (13,604)	37.8 (4688)***
Income (1-poor to 10-rich)	6.0 (1.8) ***	5.1 (1.8)	5.3 (1.8) ***
Sex (female)	51.7 (105) ns	57.3 (26,618)	46.3 (5809)***
Marital status (married & with spouse)	68.8 (137) **	55.4 (25,525	49.0 (5990)***

ns not significant, i.e., p$\geq$0.01; *p<0.01; **p<0.001; ***p<0.0001 (χ^2 for categorical, Mantel-Haenszel χ^2 for ordinal, and analysis of variance for continuous outcomes [1]applies to difference between Hindus and non-Hindus; [2]differences between all 3 groups provided for demographics; not provided are differences in religious belief/activity between non-affiliated and other groups because they are all p<0.0001 @R=religion or religious

Table 2. Comparison of beliefs, attitudes, and practices, mental health, and demographics between Hindus, members of other religious groups, and the non-affiliated: *World Values Survey 2005-2006*

	Hindus % (N)/Mean (SD)	Non-Hindus % (N)/Mean (SD)	No Affiliation % (N)/Mean (SD)
Sample size	100.0 (1,962)	100.0 (66,041)	100.0 (14,631)
Religious Beliefs			
Importance of religion			
Very important	57.4 (1,099) [ns 1]	57.1 (35,577)	7.2 (963)
Rather important	26.5 (507)	24.1 (15,447)	14.1 (1,886)
Not very important	12.0 (229)	13.7 (8,775)	35.8 (4,807)
Not at all important	4.2 (80)	5.2 (3,307)	43.0 (5,770)
Self-identification as R person			
Religious person	80.2 (1,507) [ns]	79.9 (52,079)	21.8 (3,025)
Not a religious person	17.7 (332)	18.6 (12,104)	57.1 (7,949)
A convinced atheist	2.1 (39)	1.6 (1,020)	21.1 (2,937)
Importance of God in life (1-10 scale)	7.9 (2.8) ***	8.5 (2.4)	4.3 (3.3)
Should instill R[@] faith in child at home	45.2 (887) [ns]	47.9 (32,264)	6.9 (1,013)
Religious Practices			
Active member of R organization (yes)	23.9 (468) [ns]	24.1 (15,158)	2.2 (290)
Frequency of R attendance ($\geq$once/wk)	42.6 (799) [ns]	41.3 (26,875)	2.4 (284)
Have moments of prayer or meditation	82.5 (1,574) [ns]	82.4 (47,827)	41.3 (3,960)
Demographics			
R affiliations			
Christian	0	61.4 (39,735)	0
Jewish	0	0.2 (49)	0
Islam	0	23.1 (13,962)	0
Hindu	100.0 (1,962)	0	0
Buddhist	0	4.9 (3,266)	0
Other religion	0	12.3 (7,929)	0
None	0	0	100.0 (14,631)
Age, years	40.9 (14.9) [ns]	41.4 (16.7)	42.0 (15.9) ***
Education (at least some college)	19.9 (388) [ns]	19.9 (13,339)	25.9 (3,771) ***
Income (1-10, poor to rich)	4.0 (2.2) ***	4.6 (2.3)	4.7 (2.4) ***
Sex (female)	45.0 (882) ***	53.5 (35,986)	46.5 (6,793) ***
Marital status (married)	75.5 (1,480) ***	55.4 (37,238)	50.8 (7,397) ***

[ns] not significant, i.e., p$\geq$0.01; *p<0.01; **p<0.001; ***p<0.0001, by χ^2 for categorical, Mantel-Haenszel χ^2 for ordinal, and analysis of variance for continuous outcomes
[1] applies to difference between Hindus and non-Hindus; [2] differences between all 3 groups provided for demographics and mental health; not provided are differences in religious belief/activity between non-affiliated and other groups because all are p<0.0001.   [@]R=religious or religion

World Values Survey 2005-2006 surveyed a random national sample of 83,879 adults ages 18 to 85 from more than 80 countries (approximately 1000 per country using full probability sampling). Most Hindus in this sample were from India (77.1%) or Trinidad & Tobago (11.8%). Data collection was face-to-face; carried out by an international network of social scientists, with local funding for each survey. Data were downloaded from the World Values Survey (WVS, Wave 5 2005-2008 OFFICIAL AGGREGATE v.20140429. World Values Survey Association [www.worldvaluessurvey.org]. Aggregate File Producer: Asep/JDS, Madrid SPAIN) retrieved from http://www.worldvaluessurvey.org/WVSDocumentationWV5.jsp (accessed 11-7-16)

Table 3. Comparison of beliefs and practices of Hindus with other religions and the non-affiliated: *Global Attitudes Project 2009*

Religious Beliefs	Hindus % (N)/Mean (SD)	Non-Hindus % (N)/Mean (SD)	No Affiliation % (N)/Mean (SD)
Importance of religion			
Very important	73.9 (1371) **[1]	79.4 (2576)	5.8 (39)
Somewhat important	18.0 (334)	13.1 (424)	12.1 (81)
Not important	8.1 (151)	7.5 (245)	82.0 (548)
Total	100.0 (1,856)	100.0 (3,245)	100.0 (668)
Religious Practices			
Frequency of religious attendance			
Once per week or more	34.5 (641) *	33.5 (325)	1.5 (10)
Few times/year to 1-2/month	49.2 (914)	41.9 (406)	18.9 (126)
Seldom or never	16.3 (303)	24.6 (239)	79.6 (5313)
Total	100.0 (1,858)	100.0 (970)	100.0 (667)
Frequency of prayer			
Once/day or several times/day	81.5 (1514) ***	46.3 (509)	8.1 (53)
A few times a week	8.6 (160)	14.2 (156)	3.7 (24)
Once/week or less often	9.9 (183)	39.5 (434)	88.2 (580)
Total	100.0 (1,857)	100.0 (1,099)	100.0 (657)
Demographics			
Religious affiliations			
Buddhist	0	0.3 (12)	0
Christian	0	24.5 (796)	0
Jewish	0	0.2 (9)	0
Islam	0	70.0 (2,271)	0
Hinduism	100.0 (1,858)	0	0
Sikh or Jain	0	1.2 (37)	0
Other religions	0	3.7 (120)	0
No religion	0	0	100.0 (668)
Total	100.0 (1,858)	100.0 (3,245)	100.0 (668)
Age, years	36.4 (14.3) ***	39.0 (16.1)	42.8 (16.1)***[2]
Income satisfaction (very satisfied)[3]	43.5 (812) ***	23.6 (759)	28.4 (182) ***
Sex (female)	50.4 (940) ns	53.5 (1,741)	43.8 (295) ***
Marital status (married)	62.9 (1,167) *	67.0 (2,172)	38.9 (259) ***

ns not significant, i.e., $p \geq 0.01$; *$p < 0.01$; **$p < 0.001$; ***$p < 0.0001$, by χ^2 for categorical, Mantel-Haenszel χ^2 for ordinal, and analysis of variance for continuous outcomes; not provided are differences in religious belief/activity between non-affiliated & other groups because all $p < 0.0001$. [1]difference between Hindus & non-Hindus; [2]differences between 3 groups for demograph; [3]difference largely due to low income satisfaction between Hindus in India & Muslims in Pakistan

Global Attitudes Project 2009 surveyed a random sample of 26,397 citizens ages 18 years or older from 25 countries. Information on Hindu affiliation collected in India, Great Britain, Indonesia, Pakistan, and Canada, so survey results from these countries only were included in data presented here (**97.3% of Hindus here were from India**; most non-Hindus [**67.9%**] from Pakistan and Indonesia). Data were collected by telephone and face-to-face interviews by Princeton Survey Research Associates International, as part of 2009 Pew Global Attitudes Survey. Data downloaded from the Association of Religion Data Archives, www.TheARDA.com. Pew Research Center bears no responsibility for analyses/interpretations of data presented here (11/17/16 access).

Conclusions

Hindus today have a number of distinct beliefs and practices that differentiate them from members of other religious groups. Beliefs and practices of Hindus vary to some extent depending on where in the world they live (i.e., Great Britain or South Africa vs. India). Hindus often believe in God (including belief in a personal God with whom they may relate) and religion is very important to most Hindus, sometimes more important than for members of other religious faiths. Religious practices (such as prayer, attending religious services, and having a shrine/altar/icon in their homes) are also very common among Hindus. Devout religious beliefs and practices of Hindus, then, may impact their mental health in various ways, which is the subject of the next several chapters.

CHAPTER 5

HINDUISM AND MENTAL HEALTH:

SPECULATIONS

How might the beliefs and practices of Hindus affect their mental health or influence the treatments that Hindus seek when they experience mental health problems?

Positive Effects on Mental Health

Mahatma Gandhi said: "I am a Hindu because it is Hinduism which makes the world worth living. I am a Hindu hence I love not only human beings, but all living beings" (Gandhi, 1926). Niels Bohr, who helped discover the structure of the atom, said "I go into the Upanishads to ask questions" (Prothero, 2010). Julius Robert Oppenheimer (father of the atomic bomb) said "Access to the Vedas is the greatest privilege this century may claim over all previous centuries" (Oppenheimer, 1963). American essayist Ralph Waldo Emerson said: "I owed a magnificent day to the Bhagavad Gita. It was as if an empire spoke to us, nothing small or unworthy, but large, serene, consistent, the voice of an old intelligence which in another age and climate had pondered and thus disposed of the same questions which exercise us" (Mishra, 1994).

Well-known and respected statesman, scientists, and authors, then, have inferred that Hinduism is related to good mental health, to better quality of life, and to stronger social relationships. Furthermore, there are numerous aspects of Hinduism that may link it to mental health, including an emphasis on family and community life (for most castes), an integration of religious beliefs into all of life (Hindus often say that Hinduism is not a religion but a "way of life"), an ecumenical attitude towards other religions (Hinduism accepts other religions as valid pathways to God), and a belief that everything is connected (a pantheistic view of God, but also a view of God with personal characteristics whom humans can relate to).

Specific Hindu beliefs address the relief of emotional suffering, such as an emphasis on non-attachment to material possessions and dependence on the grace of God (Lord Krishna) to take away bad karma. Such beliefs, and the practices that reinforce them, are likely to foster good mental health, peace and well-being, and facilitate coping with trauma, loss and change. The emphasis on dharma as well, where the focus is on good actions, showing kindness to others, and behaving in heroic or brave ways to protect one's family or community, could enhance social relationships and reduce stressful situations that result from self-centered greed and craving for material pleasures.

For example, the core teachings of the Bhagavad Gita focus on action in this world while at the same time emphasize avoidance of attachment to the results those actions that might cause suffering, anxiety, depression, discouragement, or otherwise adversely affect one's ability to act effectively (3:7; 3:19). Likewise, the Gita addresses the fears and anxieties that surround dying by emphasizing that death of the body is not the end:

> "There never was a time when I was not, or you, or these rulers of men. Nor will there ever be a time when we shall cease to be, all of us hereafter...It [*the eternal embodied self*] is not born, it never dies; being, it will never again cease to be. It is unborn, invariable, eternal, primeval. It is not killed when the body is killed" (2:12, 2:20).

Thus, Hindus who abide by these teachings should (at least theoretically) experience less emotional distress in whatever circumstances they may face, and consequently have better mental health.

Negative Effects on Mental Health

But, might there be anything about the Hindu belief system that could promote neurosis, mental illness, or social conflict? For example, there are many different beliefs held by Hindus, which may not always be consistent. For some, the result may be confusion about what to believe, limiting their use in coping with stress (compared to religious traditions with more set, established, agreed on beliefs). Likewise, the Hindu notion of *moksha* (non-attachment to and withdrawal from the world) may foster disengagement from friends and family, resulting in social isolation and in negative consequences for mental health (given the role that social support plays in mental health and well-being). The caste system in Hinduism may also result in the exclusion or maltreatment of members of lower castes leading to discrimination, emotional distress, and alienation of certain groups in society, resulting in mental health problems among those affected.

Another liability to mental health may involve views toward women. Early Hindu beliefs concerning the treatment of women favored the male in these ancient patriarchal societies (as in many other world religions), increasing the possibility of marital conflict or sexual coercion. For example, the Brhadaranyaka Upanishad says:

"When she has changed her clothes at the end of her menstrual period, therefore, one should approach that splendid woman and invite her to have sex. Should she refused to consent, he should bribe her. If she still refuses, he should beat her with a stick or with his fists and overpower her, saying: 'I take away the splendor from you with my virility and splendor'" (6:4:6-7).

There is evidence that such demeaning views continue to influence the treatment of women within marriage in Hindu religion majority countries such as Nepal (Puri et al., 2011) and India, where domestic violence is reported by 40% of married women (Kalokhe et al., 2015).

These findings, however, contrast with the importance of family in Hinduism and Indian culture, where sexual relations outside of marriage are less common than in any other religious groups (except for Muslims) (Adamczyk & Hayes, 2012). According to the Taittiriya Samhita (part of the Yajurveda), fidelity between husband and wife is considered the highest dharma, and according to the Mahabharata epic poem, cherishing one's wife is virtually synonymous with cherishing the goddess of prosperity (Sharma et al., 2013). However, in Indian society, there is considerable bias against women -- particularly those with mental illness, who may be abandoned by their husbands and in-laws and sent back to the homes of their parents (Sharma et al., 2013).

There is also concern that Hindu beliefs regarding karma may influence attitudes in the Hindu community toward sick people, resulting in blaming of the sick person or their family members for the illness. In a qualitative study of 29 mothers of children and adolescents with severe intellectual disability, 17 community health workers, and 16 school teachers in Vellore, India, Edwardraj and colleagues (2010) reported that cultural and Hindu religious beliefs perpetuated negative attitudes toward disability. While there was considerable dependence on personal religious faith to cope with intellectually disabled children, there were complaints of lack of organized religious support. The findings revealed that "Society did not have a positive attitude towards the family with a disabled child. People avoided them and schools blamed the parents for the problem. This was possibly due to cultural and religious beliefs that disability was due to sin committed by the parents" (p 745). Similarly, in a qualitative study involving 47 mothers of intellectually disabled children and 29 teachers in urban India, John (2012) found that "when religion is used to positively reframe the child's disability (e.g., blessing), it may be adaptive, but when it contributes to fatalistic or self-destructive beliefs (e.g., karma or punishment for past sins), it perhaps becomes maladaptive" (p 379).

A number of culture-bound syndromes in India appear to be related to Hindu religious beliefs as well. These include the Dhat syndrome (due to belief that a person needs to conserve his semen by remaining celibate if not married, and maintaining fidelity if married, which adds to his strength and brings him closer to Brahman), the possession syndrome or ghost illness (belief in possession by a religious deity or supernatural being), Bhang psychosis (also called "Indian Hemp Insanity" and due to cannabis intoxication), and Keemam dependence (addiction to indigenous product of India combined with betel leaves and lime, and chewed) (Akhtar, 1988; Freed & Freed, 1990; Prakash et al., 2014). There is also a culture-bound psychological reaction to pregnancy loss due to spontaneous abortions called Devaki syndrome (Nath et al., 2015). This involves identification with the religious figure Devaki, a Hindu queen who suffered multiple still births, but was rewarded with a child in the end (in the form of Lord Krishna). Women with this syndrome have depression and anxiety symptoms in the second trimester and become extremely preoccupied with child Krishna (and expectation of a male child). It is doubtful that Hindu beliefs are the cause of these relatively rare syndromes, which seldom occur in mentally healthy individuals.

Certain Hindu practices may also affect mental health adversely. For example, Hindu forms of intense meditation may in rare cases lead to depersonalization, dissociation, or even psychosis in vulnerable individuals (Castillo, 1990; Waelde, 2004; Kuijpers et al., 2007). Meditation when practiced alone, ego-centered, and focused entirely on enhancing well-being (as Western forms of meditation often stress, while de-emphasizing religious aspects) may lead to social isolation and excessive introversion. Finally, an unscrupulous charismatic Hindu teacher, sage, or prophet (guru) who is accountable only to self may manipulate others for self-gain, demanding humble submission or even transfer of material assets as conditions of membership in the group (Crowley & Jenkinson, 2009).

Traditional Healing Practices

Sax (2014) has written about mental health and ritual healing practices in India, which are often based on social, cultural, and religious beliefs and practices. This may involve the sick individual visiting an oracle to determine the cause of the problem and then later the seeking of a healer. The "oracle" is a person who becomes possessed by local deities and answers questions during a trance-like state. Conditions that an oracle may be consulted on include lack of energy, insomnia, sexual problems or behavioral disturbances, fear or panic, or excessive family strife. The problem is usually identified as due to strife within the family, and so the family is often the subject of the ritual healing, not the individual. This is consistent with long-held beliefs by Indians concerning the person, family, caste, and society, with the family being central. Approximately 75-80% of

Indians who seek psychiatric care in South Asia are simultaneously consulting ritual healers (Quack, 2012). Many people with mental health problems go to Hindu temples for these healing rituals. Rituals healers are typically well educated in Sanskrit, not science, and the majority of healers are low caste women or farmers.

In a study of 76 new outpatients attending a clinic in the department of psychiatry at a tertiary care hospital in Jaipur, north India, Jain and colleagues (2012) examined the route that patients usually take before finally arriving at the clinic. Family members of patients were interviewed. The majority of patients were young males from rural farming backgrounds who presented with psychotic illness. Of the five different routes that patients followed, faith healers (40%) were the most common avenue through which they ended up being referred to the psychiatry clinic (followed by allopathic medical physicians at 29%). Mean duration of illness before being seen at the psychiatric clinic was 48.8 months (over 4 years). Although 39% sought faith healers directly, 17% went to see them *after* consulting psychiatrists.

Conclusions

Hindu beliefs and practices may have either positive or negative effects as illustrated in the examples above. While it is doubtful that pathological effects on mental health are common, they bear mentioning here for completeness sake. Many of the claims above – both positive and negative reports -- are based on qualitative interviews, anecdotes or case reports. Therefore, it is time to examine what systematic quantitative research has found on the relationship between religiosity and mental health in Hindu populations (and on the mental health of Hindus compared with members of other religious groups).

CHAPTER 6

EARLY RESEARCH

Research on Hindu beliefs/practices and mental health is growing, although is still in its infancy compared to research in Christians and Muslims. Nevertheless, a number of earlier and more recent studies have sought to objectively examine these connections. Presented in this chapter is a systematic review of studies on Hindus living in India and elsewhere in the world conducted prior to 2010 (Koenig et al., 2001; 2012). In the next chapter, a selection of more recent studies published between 2010 and 2016 will be discussed, and a recent analysis of data from international surveys on Hinduism and well-being will be presented.

Reviewed now is early research (up through 2010) on the role the Hindu religion has played in coping with stress/trauma, and the relationships between religiosity/religious affiliation and coping with stress, anxiety and depression, suicide, psychosomatic symptoms, chronic mental disorder, and substance use/abuse. Studies that examine Hindu interventions to improve mental health will also be reviewed.

Coping with Stress

Dalal and Pande (1988) prospectively followed 41 patients coping with major physical injuries within the past week (21 permanently disabled). All participants were hospitalized in Allahabad, India, and most were from lower middle-class Hindu families. Participants were assessed on admission and 15 days later. When asked which among six factors was most likely to have *caused* the event, "God's will" was rated the highest. When asked which among seven factors was most essential to recovery, more than half of both permanently and temporarily disabled patients indicated "God's will." When data across the two time points in the overall sample were merged, causal attributions for the accident to karma or "God's will" were the two factors most strongly related to actual psychological recovery, especially in those who were permanently disabled (r=.43 and r=.48, respectively, on admission; r=0.29 and r=0.29 on follow-up; all p's<0.10 in this small sample).

Rammohan and colleagues (2002) examined the role that religion played in the coping of 60 Hindu family caregivers of patients with schizophrenia. Family caregiver burden was assessed using the 40-item Burden Assessment Schedule of the Schizophrenia Research Foundation. Well-being was assessed with the 28-item Psychological Well-Being Scale (Bhogle and Jaiprakash). Strength of religious belief was assessed with a single item, and numerous other coping strategies were also measured. Controlling for caregiver burden, religious belief was the strongest predictor of psychological well-being (B=0.21, p=0.01) among all coping strategies.

In a case-control study involving 62 community-dwelling Indian adults, Anjana and Raju (2003) examined the effects of reciting the Bhagavad Gita on maladjustment, finding that those who recited the Gita were more likely to be adjusted. No further details are available (only abstract available, and journal out-of-print and not accessible).

Depression

Diwan et al (2004) conducted a telephone survey of 226 migrants age 50 years or older living in the Atlanta metropolitan area. All participants had migrated from India to the U.S., and 79% were Hindu. Demographics, chronic health problems, stressful life events, mastery, religiosity, and acculturation were assessed using standard measures. Religiosity was measured by a 5-item religiosity scale that assessed frequency of meditation, prayer, reading holy books, participating in spiritual discourses, and attending religious functions. Positive and negative affect (the primary dependent variables) were measured by an 8-item version of the CESD. Results indicated that while there was no relationship between religiosity and positive affect. However, there was an inverse relationship between religiosity and negative affect/depressive symptoms ($z=-2.23$, $p=0.03$), after controlling for individual characteristics (demographics, stressful life events, chronic health problems) and personal resources (social support, mastery, acculturation).

Using a newly developed 20-item measure of Hindu religious coping (Hindu RCOPE), Tarakeshwar and colleagues (2003) examined the relationship between religious coping and mental health (depressive symptoms, life satisfaction, marital satisfaction) in 164 Hindus living in different regions of the U.S. Depressive symptoms were assessed using the CESD; life satisfaction by the Satisfaction with Life Scale; and marital satisfaction by the Kansas Marital Satisfaction Scale. The Hindu RCOPE consists of three subscales: God-focused (seeing how God might be strengthening person, seeking God's love and care, sticking to teachings and practices of religion, collaborating with God, etc.), spirituality-focused (psychophysical exercises such as yoga/meditation, seeking spiritual awakening, offering spiritual support, etc.), and negative religious coping (religious guilt, anger, and passivity). Controlling for demographic variables (age, marital status, income), the God-focused subscale was the only part of the Hindu RCOPE that was positively related to mental health (life satisfaction, $B=0.34$, $p<.01$), whereas the negative religious coping subscale (religious guilt/anger/passivity) was associated with lower life satisfaction ($B=-.27$, $p<.01$), greater depressed mood ($B=0.40$, $p<.01$), and lower marital satisfaction ($B=-0.23$, $p<.05$).

Suicide

Suicide rates can serve as a proxy for mental health, although cultural factors also play a role (i.e., suicide may be more permissible in certain religions, especially Eastern religious belief systems). The government of India published a report on suicide rate in 1964-1965, indicating a rate of 5.7-6.3/100,000, which was considerably lower than that for the United States (11.1/100,000) and many other countries at the time (Pandey, 1968). In explaining the results,

Pandey argued that while Hindus do not believe that suicide brings eternal damnation, they do believe that the spirit of the person who committed suicide remains on the earth until the period of their granted lifetime ends and suffers pains more severe than a usual death would bring. After that period ends, it is believed that the person will be reborn into the same, higher, or lower "form" depending on past actions (karma), of which the act of the suicide is only one. Pandey explains how Hindus of the time understood suicide, based on the "theory of the gunas" (as described in chapters 3, 7, 13, 14, 17 and 18 of the Bhagavad Gita). The belief is that most suicides are committed when the Tamas guna has more sway over the person's life than other gunas:

> The theory of the gunas, which describes all human behavior, is known by every Hindu. The gunas represent different stages in evolution in any particular eternity. They are also understood in terms of personal qualities endowed by the Almighty. Every person is born with some combination of the gunas. The relative dominance of the gunas may change in the course of a person's life depending upon his actions, committed either in this or a past life. The three gunas are Sattwa, Rajas, and Tamas. They come from Prakriti (the Cosmos) which is of eightfold composition: earth, water, fire, air, ether, mind, intellect, and ego. Sattwa has the element of sacrifice, and it is the light which makes men search for knowledge, wisdom, happiness, and contentment. Rajas has the element of greed, and it has a stimulating nature which makes individuals thirsty for pleasure, power, and possession. Tamas, the affecting factor which darkens the judgment of the doer, has the elements of delusion, sluggishness, and stupor... When Sattwa prevails over Rajas and Tamas, the man is happy, contented, and understanding. When Rajas dominates over Sattwa and Tamas, the person feels lustful for power and possession, is very greedy and restless. If Tamas rules over the other two gunas, the person is lost in the dark, bewildered, slothful and deluded (pp 199-200).

Thus, when the Tamas gunas is strong in a person's life, this state of darkness and delusion increases the risk for suicide.

Kamal and Lowenthal (2002) examined the relationship between religiosity and suicide beliefs/behaviors among 40 Hindus and 60 Muslims (mean age 22.5 years) living in the greater London area (UK). Religiosity was assessed by frequency of prayer, religious study, and attendance at worship services. Suicidal beliefs and behavior were assessed using the 47-item Reasons for Living Inventory (RLI), which has six subscales assessing survival and coping, importance of family, importance of having children, fear of suicide, fear of social disapproval, and moral reasons. In addition frequency of suicidal thoughts, suicidal plans, and suicide attempts were also assessed. Results indicated that Muslims were significantly more likely than Hindus to endorse moral, survival/coping beliefs, and overall reasons for living. However, there were no significant differences between Muslims and Hindus on suicidal thoughts, plans or behavior. Religious activity overall did not correlate with any RFL subscale (except the moral reasons subscale), and did not correlate with suicidal thoughts, plans or behavior.

In contrast, a survey of adolescents in Delhi, India, found an increased risk of suicidal tendencies among Hindus (Sidhartha and Jena, 2006). These researchers surveyed 1205 adolescents ages 12 to 19 years attending two schools in central Delhi examining the prevalence and predictors of non-fatal suicidal behaviors (NFSB) across the lifetime and during the past year. Adolescents were 85% Hindu, 8% Muslim, 6% Jains, and 0.7% Christian. Results indicated that lifetime prevalence of suicidal ideation was 21.7% and past year suicidal ideation was 11.7%; prevalence of lifetime suicide attempt was 8% and past year suicide attempt was 3.5%. Significant predictors of NFSB were female gender, older age, history of physical abuse by parents, feeling neglected, running away from school, suicide by friend, death wish, deliberate self-harm, and Hindu religion (OR=1.67, 95% CI 1.09-2.57).

The findings above conflict with those reported by Gururaj and colleagues (2004), who conducted a case-control study involving interviews with families of 269 persons who had completed suicides and 259 living controls from the same community (Bangalore). Cases and controls were matched on age and gender. The majority of suicides occurred between the ages of 16 and 39 (67%) and among those with relatively low education (84% with 10th grade or less). *Lack of* religious beliefs predicted a nearly 20-fold increase in likelihood of suicide (OR=19.2, p<0.001).

Anxiety and Fear

In an early study of religiosity and psychological symptoms in India, Hassan and Khalique (1981) surveyed a random sample of 480 college students in Ranchi and Jamshedpur, India, (160 Hindu males, 160 Hindu females, 160 Muslim males, 160 Muslim females), examining the relationship between religiosity, anxiety, authoritarianism, rigidity, and intolerance of ambiguity. A 10-item religiosity scale constructed by the investigators was administered, along with measures of authoritarianism, rigidity, intolerance of ambiguity, and anxiety (using standard scales of these constructs). Results indicated that religiosity was higher among Muslims compared to Hindus (35.5 vs. 29.9, p=0.01), was not related to caste level (high vs. low), but was *positively* related to authoritarianism (r=0.34, p<.01), anxiety (r=0.46, p<.01), rigidity (r=0.48, p<.01), and intolerance of ambiguity (r=0.54, p<.01). Researchers concluded that "It may be that religiosity is a kind of defensive reaction against personality weakness" (p 134).

In what may be the first experimental study to examine the effects of religiosity on mental health in India, Dhawan and Sripat (1986) examined the effects of religiosity on fear of death in 100 undergraduate students, 40 of whom were divided into high (n=20) and low (n=20) religiosity groups based on the Bhushan's religiosity scale (1970). Fear of death (assessed by Sinha's Threat Perception Scale) was induced in half of subjects by exposing them to fear of death cards, thus creating four groups: 10 religious fear-exposed subjects (A), 10 non-religious fear-exposed subjects (B), 10 religious controls (C), and 10 non-religious controls (D). Need for affiliation with others (assessed by Murray's TAT Card Test) in response fear of death was also assessed. Results indicated that fear of death and need for affiliation were significantly higher in the experimental groups (A and B) compared to controls (C and D), as expected. Religiosity, however, was not related to fear of death nor did it reduce fear of death or subsequent affiliation behavior in the experimental group.

Guglani et al (2000) examined relationship between religiosity and mental health in 70 Hindu grandmothers (mean age 66.9 years) as part of a study of Asian families living in the United Kingdom (UK). Grandmothers had lived an average of 23.0 years in the UK. Religiosity was assessed using a 12-item Hindu religious participation scale that assessed level of devotion, frequency of religious attendance, and frequency of other organized religious activity.

Mental health measures included the 14-item Hospital Anxiety and Depression Scale and the 10-item Rosenberg Self-Esteem Scale. Uncontrolled analyses indicated no significant relationship between religious participation and anxiety, depression, or self-esteem.

Somatic/Psychosomatic Symptoms

In one of the first studies to examine religion and mental health among Hindus, De Figueiredo and Lemkau (1978) surveyed a stratified random sample of adults in Goa, India, in 1973. Participants were 80 Christians and 80 Hindus of similar education, occupation and income. Among Hindus, 43% attended temple once/week or more compared to 46% of Christians who attended religious services more than once/week, while 65% of Hindus "often" engaged in private worship at home (prayer or scripture reading) compared to 50% of Christians. A 23-item measure of psychosomatic symptoms was used to assess sleep quality, mood, concentration, and other psychological and somatic symptoms. Results indicated that Christians and Hindus had a similar level of psychosomatic symptoms, but those with high religious attendance (vs. low) were significantly less likely to experience high levels of psychosomatic symptom. Among Christians, this was true for both men (2.5% vs. 15.0%, p=0.016) and women (2.5% vs. 32.5%, p=0.0002). Among Hindus, this was true for women (10.0% vs. 50.0%, p=0.001) but not for men (10.0% vs. 25.0%, p=0.24). For private religiousness, however, the pattern was reversed. Among Christians, high prayer and scripture reading (vs. low) were associated with high psychosomatic symptoms in both men (15.0% vs. 2.5%, p=0.007) and women (30.0% vs. 5.0%, p=0.0005). Among Hindus, this was true in men (30.0% vs. 2.5%, p=0.02) and a similar trend was present in women (40.0% vs. 20.0%, p=0.08). These findings provide a mixed picture on religiosity and psychosomatic symptoms.

Next, Chaturvedi and Bhandari (1989) examined illness behavior patterns in 31 consecutively admitted psychiatric outpatients in Bangalore, India, who (1) volunteered a complaint of pain or other bodily symptom, (2) had organic pathology excluded by detailed physical exam, (3) had a duration of illness greater than 6 months, (4) were previously treated by a medical physician for their complaints, and (5) had more than two somatic symptoms for which no organic basis could be found. Results indicated that Hindus (n=24) were more likely to recall they were told they had physical illness compared with Muslims (n=7) (p<0.004), and to believe that the cause of their psychiatric illness was physical in nature (p=0.03). Researchers concluded that Hindus were more likely to demonstrate "denial" and exhibit greater somatization (believed they had physical causes for their psychiatric illness).

Although not strictly considered psychosomatic, eating disorders are conditions involving strong somatic preoccupation. Therefore, information about such conditions in Hindus may help to clarify the link with somatization described by Chaturvedi and Bhandari (1989) above. In a study that assessed religion and eating disorders, Bhugra and colleagues (2000) found no association between the presence of bulimic symptoms (assessed using the 26-item BITE) and religious affiliation (87.9% Hindu, 9.5% Sikh, 0.8% Muslim) in a sample of 504 students at an all-girl college in northern India.

Patel and colleagues (2006) examined the relationship between religious affiliation and complaints of abnormal vaginal discharge (AVD) among a random sample of 2,094 community dwelling women ages 18-45 years living in the state of Goa, India (75% Hindu, 22% Christian, 3% Muslim). AVD is known to be a common psycho-somatic complaint in this region of India. Somatic symptoms were assessed with a 20-item Scale for Somatic Symptoms, and mental health was determined by the Revised Clinical Interview Schedule. Participants were assessed at three periods T0 (baseline), T1 (six months), and T2 (12 months). The incidence of AVD during each of the two time periods (T0-T1 and T1-T2) was 3.6% and 4.0%. Factors associated with complaint of AVD in a multivariate model were younger age, illiteracy, concern that husband having extra-marital affairs, high somatic symptom scores, poor mental health, current bacterial vaginosis, and being Muslim (OR=3.2, CI 1.7-6.0) or Christian (OR=1.6, 95% CI 1.0-2.3), compared with being Hindu. Thus, Hindus had the lowest incidence of AVD. Also, see results of a Hindu-based intervention below showing a reduction in menopausal symptoms that may have a psychosomatic component (Chattha et al., 2008). Thus, there is only minimal evidence that Hindus express more psychosomatic symptoms than non-Hindus.

Schizophrenia

In the first known longitudinal study of religion and mental health in Hindus, Verghese and colleagues (1989) conducted a 2-year prospective study of 323 persons with schizophrenia ages 15-45 within two year of diagnosis seen at university psychiatric outpatient clinics in, Lucknow, Madras, and Vellore, India. Symptoms were assessed using the Present State Exam (a well-known structured psychiatric interview). Examined were factors associated with a good overall outcome at 2-year follow-up. Of the 10 factors associated with good overall outcome, an increase in religious activities was one ($p<0.001$). Investigators concluded that "If these associations are confirmed, it is possible to plan some intervention programs, such as changing the attitudes of others to the patient, and giving more importance to various types of religious activity. Religiosity is important in Indian culture and the increase in religiosity that was related to better outcome in the present study could be a means of effectively handling the anxiety of the patient" (p 502).

Thara and Eaton (1996) followed 76 patients with chronic schizophrenia in Madras, India, for 10 years examining predictors of clinical outcome. Outcomes were categorized into "good" or "poor," where poor involved relapses and continuous illness. Diagnosis and outcomes were again based on the Present State Exam and clinical course. Although religious activity did not differ between the two outcomes, those with religious and grandiose delusions were over nine times more likely to be in the poor outcome group (adjusted OR=9.21, $p<0.01$). Unfortunately, religious and grandiose delusions were combined into a single category, making it difficult to determine if increased risk was due specifically to religious delusions or to grandiose delusions.

In a study that was largely qualitative, Kulhara et al (2000) examined religious attitudes toward illness and treatment in 40 patients with schizophrenia and relatives (70% Hindus, 26% Sikhs) attending a psychiatric outpatient clinic in Northern India. Although most patients had hallucinations (70%) and delusions (92%), only 10% had religious delusions. Of those with delusions, 38% express them in terms of paranormal phenomena. Patients' relatives were asked about magical-religious beliefs as the cause of the mental illness. Over one-third (35%) attributed the illness to sorcery, 25% to ghost/evil spirits,

25% to spirit intrusion, 16% to evil spirits, and 12% to divine wrath. Nearly half of relatives (46%) indicated that such beliefs were prevalent in the community to which they belonged (these relatives were urban-dwelling and well-educated). One-third of relatives (33%) expressed the belief that performance of religious rituals (puja) or magical-religious rituals (Jhad-Phoonk) could improve the patient's condition, 53% said they had consulted a faith healer or a priest, and 58% said that religious rituals had been performed during the present illness. Researchers concluded that belief in supernatural influences is common among relatives of patients with schizophrenia, even those from urban areas with fairly high education.

In one of the most remarkable studies published to date, investigators from the National Institute of Mental Health and Neurosciences, Bangalore, India, examined the effects of staying at a Hindu temple in 31 psychotic patients (23 paranoid schizophrenia, 6 delusional disorder, 2 bipolar disorder in manic phase) (Raguram et al., 2002). No participants received medical care from a psychiatrist either prior to or during the stay at the temple. The temple was located in the village of Velayuthampalayampudur, Dindugal District, Tamil Nadu, and was built over the tomb of a mentally ill person said to have had healing powers (for mental illnesses in particular). Families for years had brought their mentally ill relatives to stay in the temple and took care of their daily needs. During their temple stay, the mentally ill were encouraged to take part in the daily routines of the temple, such as cleaning the compound, watering the plants, and other maintenance activities. Consecutive patients who came to the temple for help over a 3-month period were studied. The Brief Psychiatric Rating Scale (BPRS), which assesses 18 psychiatric symptoms, was administered by a psychiatrist on admission to the temple and just prior to leaving the temple. Average length of stay was six weeks (range 1-24 weeks). Outcomes were clinical symptoms on BPRS and perceived benefit reported by family members. Results indicated a 20% drop in BPRS score from 52.9 on admission to 42.9 on departure ($p < 0.001$). According to subjective evaluation by family caregivers, 22 subjects (71%) had improved and three had fully recovered. Investigators noted that a 20% change in the BPRS (as noted with these patients) is similar to that seen with psychotropic drugs, including newer atypical antipsychotics.

Drug Use/Abuse

Dube and colleagues (1975) examined cannabis use and religious affiliation among all male first admissions to a psychiatric hospital in Agra, India (n=566). Hindus were more likely to be cannabis users than were Muslims (25.8% vs. 3.8%). This was particularly true among the Kshatriyas warrior caste (30.6%) and only slightly lower (24.0%) among the Brahmin caste (priests and nobles). The next study examined opium use in a random sample of 2,064 men and 1,536 women age 15 or over in Punjab, India (Mohan et al., 1979). Among men, religious affiliation was a significant predictor of opium use, with Sikhs more likely to use opium than Hindus, and Hindus more likely to use opium than other religious groups (11.7% vs. 5.3% vs 1.9%, p<.001, respectively).

Chaturvedi and colleagues (2003) surveyed a random sample of 1,831 community-dwelling persons ages 10 and above (mean age 30.2 years) from two selected states in Northeast India. Participants were 77% Hindu, 21% Christian, and 2% Muslim. Tobacco use by religion was 42.8% among Christians (21.5% chewers and 22.8% smokers) and 25.9% among Hindus (20.4% chewers and 9.9% smokers). Christians were more likely to be cigarette smokers (22.8%) then were Muslims (14.8%) or Hindus (9.9%).

Alcohol Use/Abuse

Chaturvedi et al (2003) found no differences in use of alcohol between Christian, Muslim, and Hindu adults (12.8%, 7.4%, and 12.5%, respectively). Among youth, however, the findings have been different – at least among Hindu youth living outside of India. Bradby and Williams (2006) examined the relationship between religious affiliation and substance use among 824 South Asian adolescents ages 14-15 and 18-20 years living in the greater Glasgow area (Scotland). A goal of the study was to examine the influence of religious affiliation on change in alcohol use, cigarette smoking, and illicit drug use from high school to after high school graduation. Unfortunately, this study compared two separate cohorts rather than prospectively following a single cohort. Participants were 47% Muslim, 10% Sikhs/Hindu, and 43% Christian. Results indicated that Muslims were nearly always less likely than Sikhs/Hindus to have tried alcohol or to be current drinkers. Sikh/Hindu women, however, reported less experimentation with tobacco than did Muslim women.

Christians were more likely to report ever having experimented with and currently drinking alcohol, smoking cigarettes, or using illicit drugs than either Muslims or Sikhs/Hindus. However, increases in use from high school to afterward graduation appeared to be largest among Sikh/Hindu males.

Rollocks and Dass (2007) examined the effects of religious affiliation on alcohol use and alcohol attitudes among 380 male and 455 female adolescent ages 13 to 18 years attending high schools in the West Indies. Participants consisted of 44% Christians, 11% Hindus, 6% Muslims, and 39% other religious groups. Uncontrolled results indicated that regular use of alcohol was higher among Hindus than other religious groups (p<0.003), although there was no difference in age at first use or attitudes toward use.

Religious Interventions
At least four clinical trials have examined the effects of Hindu religious interventions on mental health outcomes, all reporting significant benefits.

In a single-group experimental study, Mohan et al (2004) examined the effects of a spiritually-based lifestyle change program (developed by Rishi Samskruit Vidya Kendra) on well-being. Although details are lacking due to inability to access the report, results indicated that the overwhelming majority of 200 participants experienced an increase in their sense of purpose/meaning and in their need to achieve higher consciousness.

Harinath and colleagues (2004) examined the effects of Hatha yoga and Omkar meditation on the mental health of a sample of 30 healthy males aged 25-35 years randomized to either the intervention or a control group. In the morning, participants in the intervention group practiced yogic postures for 45 minutes and pranayama (forcefully expiring the breath, breathing air through teeth, alternate nostril breathing, making buzzing sounds with closed lips) for 15 minutes; in the evening, they practiced yogic postures for 15 minutes, pranayama for 15 minutes, and meditation (Omkar meditation, i.e., the Om chant) for 30 minutes. These activities were practiced daily for 3 months. Those in the control group performed body flexibility exercises for 40 minutes and running for 20 minutes in the morning and played games for 60 minutes in the evening. Outcomes were anxiety (IPAT Anxiety Scale), depressive symptoms (MMPI), and well-being (50-item scale developed by authors). No significant within group changes in anxiety or depression were found from before to afterwards for either the intervention or the control group, although well-being increased significantly in the intervention group ($p < 0.001$) compared to no change in the control group (post-intervention between group differences were not reported).

Chattha and colleagues (2008) conducted a randomized clinical trial to examine the effects of an integrated yoga intervention on menopausal symptoms among 120 women in Bangalore, India. Menopausal women ages 45-55 years were randomized to either a yoga intervention or a control group. The yoga intervention was based on the original Patanjali yoga sutras and Mandukaya Karika scriptures and consisted of slowing down the flow of thoughts, yogic breathing practices, and simple body movements. These were practiced over 8 weeks. The control group practiced a set of exercises consisting of body movements for one hour daily for five days per week for 8 weeks. Controls received a similar numbers of lectures, and a similar amount of time was spent in individual counseling compared to the intervention group. A total of 54 participants in each group completed the clinical trial. No differences in menopausal symptoms or other characteristics were present at baseline between groups. Outcome measures included the Green Climacteric Scale for psychological, somatic, and vasomotor symptoms, the Perceived Stress Scale, and the Eysenck's Personality Inventory (assessing extroversion vs. neuroticism). Results indicated a marginally significant between-group difference on psychological symptoms ($p = 0.06$), somatic symptoms ($p = 0.19$), and vasomotor symptoms ($p = 0.03$), all favoring the intervention group. Perceived stress ($p < 0.001$) and neuroticism scores ($p < 0.05$) were also significantly lower in the intervention compared to the control group.

Finally, Satyapriya and colleagues (2009) conducted a randomized clinical trial involving 90 pregnant women in Bangalore, India. Participants in their 18th-20th week of pregnancy were randomized to either an integrated yoga therapy group or a control group (standard prenatal exercises). As in the Chattha et al (2008) study above, those in the yoga intervention group participated yoga based on Hindu scriptures (Patanjali yoga sutras), which consisted of physical postures (asanas) and breathing techniques (pranayama) to improve flexibility, balance, and vital energy (prana). The intervention included meditation (slowing down the flow of thoughts) and relaxation techniques, such as the isomeric relaxation. In the first month, both intervention and control groups received instructions from trainers during 2-hour sessions 3 days per week; for the next three months, women practiced for 1 hour per day at home. In addition, both intervention and control groups had 1-hour refresher classes at each prenatal visit every 4 weeks up to the 28th week and every 2 weeks up to the 36th week. Results at the end of the trial indicated that participants in the intervention group experienced a significant reduction in stress symptoms on the Perceived Stress Scale (between-group differences significant at $p=0.001$), which was the only psychological outcome measured. Not clear was the extent to which participants in the control group received equal social attention as those in the intervention group.

Conclusions

This systematic review of quantitative (and some qualitative) research conducted up through 2010 examined studies that compared Hindus and non-Hindus on mental health (and substance use), explored the relationship between religiosity and mental health in Hindus, and examined the effects of Hindu interventions on mental health outcomes (go to Chapter 8 to see an overall summary of the research findings). One thing is for certain. Hindus often use their religious beliefs to cope with stress; Hindus often explain mental illness in religious terms; and religious treatments are often sought for mental conditions.

CHAPTER 7

LATEST RESEARCH

To give a sense of the volume of published studies since 2010, a literature search using the words Hinduism and mental health in Google Scholar (9/8/16) yielded almost 18,000 results. Only a small fraction of these, however, were quantitative studies comparing Hindus and non-Hindus or examining relationships between religiosity and mental health in Hindus. To conduct a systematic review of even this small literature (like we conducted in the last chapter for research published prior to 2010), however, is beyond the scope of this review. Instead, a sampling of more recent studies will now be presented that illustrates the types of studies that have been appearing in the literature since 2010.

Research in this area has been held back in part by the lack of reliable/valid measures of Hindu religiosity. Although at least three such measures have been published (Bhushan scale, Hindu RCOPE, and Santosh-Francis Attitude toward Hinduism Scale), these scales assess religiosity quite broadly and often do not assess specific Hindu beliefs and practices (Bhushan, 1970; Tarakeshwar et al., 2003; Francis et al., 2008). Perhaps lack of specificity is necessary given the wide range of beliefs and practices in the Hindu faith tradition.

Studies from the research reviewed above will be categorized into coping with stress, anxiety and depression, suicide, somatic/psychosomatic symptoms, chronic mental illness, and substance abuse. In addition, research on psychological well-being will be included given the dramatic increase in research in the area of positive psychology. Recent Hindu-based mental health interventions (excluding studies of western-based Transcendental Meditation) will also be examined.

Coping with Stress

In a study of Hindu family caregivers of patients with cancer in Pune, India, Thombre and colleagues (2010) found that positive religious coping was associated with increased post-traumatic growth (PTG) and PTG was associated with less use of negative coping strategies. The authors concluded that these findings underscored the importance of meaning-focused forms of religious coping.

In a qualitative study of 18 first-generation Asian Indian older adults ages 61 to 82 years who had emigrated from India to the US, Tummala-Narra and colleagues (2012) found that spirituality or belief in a higher power helped to explain reasons for situations and events, including integration to the U.S. Since all participants were Hindus, researchers speculated that karma (belief that actions in the past determine future events) may have contributed to their ability to make sense of life transitions at this time. In particular the Hindu belief in contemplating life and death during the last stages of life seemed to drive their reminiscing about past life events and putting them in perspective (which researchers indicated was healthy).

Benson and colleagues (2012) examined the relationship between religious coping and enculturation stress in 112 Hindu Bhutanese refugees from camps in Nepal, who were now settled in Phoenix, Arizona. Over half had little or no English proficiency and few had any formal schooling. Using the 20-item Hindu RCOPE and two standard scales of acculturation stress, researchers found that contrary to expectation, higher religious coping was associated with *higher levels* of acculturation stress, both environmental ($r=0.47$, $p<0.01$) and social ($r=0.46$, $p<0.01$). These associations remained significant after controlling for age, education, marital status, working status, English proficiency, and satisfaction with social support. The authors explained that participating in ethnic communities (reflected by high levels of Hindu religious coping) may have an "insulating or cocooning effect" that could hinder the acculturation process for these refugees. An alternative explanation, not mentioned by the authors, is that high acculturation stress could have caused these refugees to turn to their religious beliefs for comfort and meaning.

Shah and colleagues (2011a) examined the relationship between religious/spiritual (R/S) beliefs and coping among 103 outpatients with residual schizophrenia (mean age 34.4) in Chandigarh, India. Mood symptoms were assessed by the Positive and Negative Syndrome Scale (PANSS), and coping behaviors were measured by the Ways of Coping Checklist (WCC). R/S was assessed using the WHO Quality of Life-Spirituality, Religiousness and Personal Beliefs scale (SRPB), which measures spirituality, spiritual connection, meaning and purpose, experiences of awe and wonder, wholeness and integration, spiritual strength, inner peace, hope, optimism, and faith (i.e., this scale is heavily contaminated by indicators of mental health). The "faith" subscale asks: "To what extent does faith contribute to your well-being?"; "To what extent does faith give you comfort in daily life?"; "To what extent does faith give you strength in daily life?"; and "To what extent does faith help you to enjoy life?" While the "faith" subscale is the least contaminated with mental health items and most distinctive of the eight subscales, it is still heavily loaded with items tapping good mental health. Furthermore, how this patients understood the word "faith" is also unclear. Nevertheless, higher SRPB scores overall were associated with greater distancing, self-control, problem-solving, and positive appraisal. The faith subscale of the SRPB was positively associated with confrontational (r=0.27, p<0.01) and positive appraisal (r=0.44, p<0.001), both healthy coping strategies. No correlation was found between SRPB and mood scores on the PANSS.

In a second report from this study, Kate et al (2013) examined 100 caregivers of patients with schizophrenia to identify factors associated with positive aspects of caregiving. The Scale for Positive Aspects of Caregiving Experience (SPACE) assessed the primary outcome. All subscales of the SRPB (except meaning/ purpose) including the faith subscale were positively associated with positive aspects of caregiving (r=0.23, p=0.02). Given the contaminated measures of spirituality used here, not much can be said about either the coping of Hindus with schizophrenia or their caregivers.

Depression

Gupta and colleagues (2011) examined relationships between religiosity and psychopathology in 60 patients experiencing a depressive disorder for the first time. Participants were being seen at a psychiatry clinic in Chandigarh, North India. Depression was assessed by the Beck Depression Inventory (BDI) and by the Hamilton Depression Rating Scale (HDRS). Also assessed were hopelessness (Beck Hopelessness Scale) and suicidal intent (10-item scale). Religiosity was measured in the local language using a 44-item scale which measured level of religious faith and belief. Based on their score, participants were divided into low (n=30) and high (n=30) religious groups. Although trends were in the expected direction, no significant difference was found between high and low religious groups on depressive symptoms or level of hopelessness or suicidal ideation. However, religiosity overall was inversely related to hopelessness on the Beck scale (r=-0.31, p<0.05) and to suicidal ideation (r=-0.35, p<0.01). Researchers concluded that "In depressed patients, hopelessness and suicidal intent are inversely related to level of religiosity."

Agrawal and colleagues (2011) examined religious affiliation, and psychological well-being in 1,099 adults in Bangalore, South India (89% Hindu). Well-being was assessed with the 26-item PANAS (assessing positive and negative affect) and with Diener's 5-item Satisfaction with Life Scale. No difference was found in positive affect or life satisfaction between Hindus and non-Hindus (mostly Christians and Muslims); however, negative affect was significantly lower among Hindus (p<0.05). Step-wise regression analyses controlling for income, age, and work status confirmed this relationship (B=0.07, p=0.025), which was similar in both men and women (though somewhat stronger in women).

Chokkanathan (2013) examined the relationship between religiosity and depressive symptoms in a random sample of 312 Hindu adults age 65 or older living in Chennai (Madras), India. Religiosity was measured using the 5-item Duke University Religion Index (DUREL), consisting of three subscales (ORA=organizational religiosity, NORA=non-organizational religiosity, IR=intrinsic religiosity). Also assessed were social support, depressive symptoms (20-item CESD and 15-item GDS), and mastery (6-item Pearlin scale). Simple correlations revealed a significant and inverse relationship between all three religious subscales and both measures of depressive symptoms, and a positive relationship between IR and mastery. Structural equation modeling was used to examine all relationships simultaneously. Religiosity was inversely related to depression both directly (B=-0.30, p<0.05) and indirectly (B=-0.14), producing a significant total inverse correlation (B=-0.44, p<0.01). Researchers concluded that "These findings suggest the crucial role of religiosity in influencing the well-being of older adults. The need to integrate religiosity in interventions for older Indian adults is discussed" (p 880).

Those with depression often have poor self-esteem and score low on self-efficacy. Khan and colleagues (2014) examined the association between religious practices, social identification as Hindu, self-efficacy, and well-being in 792 Hindu participants living in a rural area in northern India (Allahabad). The average age of participants was 64.1 years; 47% were female; and 91% belong to the general caste. Self-efficacy was assessed using a 5-item standard scale (e.g., able to manage life, capable of doing things that matter, in control of life), and well-being was measured by a 3-item scale that assessed how often participants felt anxious, restless, and irritable. A 6-item religious practices scale measured religious practices at home (how often participants performed morning prayers, evening prayers, chanted religious texts) and religious practices at the temple (attended temple, offered gifts at temple, read or chanted religious texts at temple). Social identification as Hindu was assessed by three questions: "Does being Hindu matter to you?"; "Is being Hindu a key part of your life?"; and "Is being Hindu central to your sense of who you are?" Results indicated that self-efficacy was associated with religious practices at home (r=0.20, p<0.001), religious practices at temple (r=0.14, p<0.001), and social identification as Hindu (r=0.27, p<0.001). Religious practices at home were associated with fewer negative psychological symptoms (r=-0.14, p<0.001), although no significant relationship was found with religious practices at temple or social identification as Hindu. Structural equation modeling, however, indicated that social identification as Hindu was the only religious factor that independently predicted self-efficacy (B=0.14, p<0.001). Because of its relationship to self-efficacy, identification as Hindu was also related indirectly to better psychological and physical health.

Kamble and colleagues (2014) examined the relationship between religiosity and psychological adjustment in 250 graduate students at Karnatak University in Dharwad, India. Religiosity was measured by the 19-item Santosh-Francis Attitude toward Hinduism Scale (ATHS) and by a version of the Gorsuch and McPherson religious orientation scale that assesses intrinsic (IR), extrinsic religiosity-personal (ER-P), and extrinsic religiosity-social (ER-S). In addition, the 12-item Quest Scale (QS) (Batson) and the 16-item Religious Collective Self-Esteem Scale (RCSES) were also administered. Mental health characteristics assessed were self-esteem (assessed by 10-item Rosenberg scale) and depression/anxiety (assessed by Costello & Comrey scales). Regression analysis revealed that ATHS was positively associated with self-esteem (B=0.14, $p<0.01$) and negatively associated with depression (B=-0.10, $p<0.05$), and there was a significant interaction between ATHS and IR such that participants who scored high on both scales had especially high self-esteem (B=0.11, $p<0.001$), low levels of depression (B=-0.10, $p<0.001$), and low anxiety (B=-0.08, $p<0.01$).

Finally, in a study of 104 patients with HIV/AIDS being seen in a specialty clinic in Uttar Pradesh, India, Rai and Verma (2015) examined the relationship between religious affiliation (88.5% Hindu, 11.5% Muslim) and depression using the GHQ-28 and Montgomery-Asberg Depression Rating Scale (MADRS). The prevalence of depression (67.3%) and anxiety (76.9%) were high in this sample, with nearly two-thirds having CD4 counts of less than 300 (getting close to the threshold for having AIDS, which is < 200). Hindus were significantly more likely than Muslims to experience depression (70.7% vs. 41.7%, $p<0.05$).

Suicide

Recall from the last chapter that earlier research had indicated low rates of suicide in India, considerably lower than in the U.S. and rest of the world (Pandey, 1968). More recent research, however, suggests that the suicide rate has been increasing in India. Between 1987 and 2007, the suicide rate increased from 7.9 to 10.3 per 100,000 (Vijaykumar, 2007), and remained stable at 10.5 per 100,000 in 2009 (Varnik, 2012). However, in 2012, the World Health Organization reported that India had the highest number of suicides in the world with a suicide rate of 21.1 per 100,000. This was not the highest suicide rate in the world, but given the large population of India, no other country had more suicides (WHO, 2014). The rate appears especially high among women, where in 2012 the suicide rate was the 6th highest of any country (vs. 22nd highest for males). This is despite the fact that up until 2014, suicide was considered a criminal act under the Indian penal code. Because of that, rates prior to 2014 were often underestimated due to poor civil registration, variable standards in certifying deaths, legal problems, and stigma (Gupta et al., 2015). A number of recent studies have examined the relationship between Hindu religious affiliation or religiosity in Hindus and suicidal thoughts, attempts, or completed suicide.

Sisask and colleagues (2010) examined whether religiosity was a protective factor against attempted suicide. Analyzing data from the World Health Organization's Suicide Prevention-Multisite Intervention Study on Suicidal Behaviors, suicide attempters were identified in seven countries: Brazil, Estonia, India, Islamic Republic of Iran, South Africa, Sri Lanka, and Vietnam. Suicide attempters were compared with controls from the general population. Religious characteristics were assessed, including religious affiliation, frequency of religious attendance, and self-identification as a religious person. In India, 571 suicide attempters were identified and compared to 460 controls from the general population. Suicide attempters were less likely to be Hindu-affiliated compared to those in the general population (84.0% vs. 92.0%); this trend was also true for the country of Sri Lanka (10.3% vs. 17.5%). In India, compared to those who never attended religious services, those who attended religious services yearly were at lower risk for suicide attempt (OR=0.45, 95% CI 0.26-0.77), controlling for gender, age, marriage, employment, and education. Self-identification as a religious person, though, was not related to suicide attempt.

Manoranjtham and colleagues (2010) examined risk factors for suicide in rural south India (Vellore district). A total of 100 consecutive suicides were compared with 100 living controls matched for age, gender, and neighborhood. First-degree relatives of the 100 suicide cases were interviewed for this study. Bivariate analyses indicated that lack of religious faith was more likely in suicide cases than controls (27% vs. 14%, OR=2.3, 95 CI 1.1-4.7, p<0.05). In multivariate analyses, the only significant predictors of suicide were "ongoing stress" and chronic pain. The authors concluded that in India, many suicides were impulsive and related to stress. They also indicated that earlier qualitative analyses had revealed attitudes in the general population toward suicide. Many considered suicide a viable option when faced with insoluble personal difficulties and misfortune (Manoranjitham et al, 2007). Researchers also indicated that suicide in India is more likely due to stress and conflict (social, economic and cultural factors) than to mental illness, and underscored the belief that suicides are likely under-reported due to social stigma and legal consequences (as noted earlier; although I suspect that the decriminalization of suicide in 2014 may have reduced under-reporting to some extent).

Stack & Kposowa (2011) examined the relationship between suicide acceptability and religious affiliation/religiosity using data from the 1999-2001 World Values Survey that assessed 50,547 participants in 56 countries. Religious commitment was measured by religious orthodoxy and attendance at religious services; religious *networks* by time spent with co-religionists; and religious coping by dependence on religion to cope. Results indicated an inverse relationship between Hindu religious affiliation and acceptability of suicide (B=-0.119, p<0.01), although this was the weakest inverse correlation when compared to inverse correlations with Muslim, Buddhist, Protestant, Catholic, Orthodox, and other affiliations. The inverse relationship with Hindu affiliation diminished to non-significance when religious commitment and religious networks were controlled for and remained nonsignificant when analyses were further controlled for moral community theory, national religious attendance, GDP per capita, and sociodemographic characteristics.

Similar findings were reported by Boyd and Chung (2012) who examined the same suicide variable using data from the 2005 World Values Survey (n=42,299 persons from 43 countries), where suicide acceptability was rated on a scale from 1-10 (1=never justifiable; 10= always justifiable). Religious measures were attendance at religious services (never to once a week) and importance of religion in life (not at all important to very important), along with religious affiliation. Multilevel modeling was used to analyze the data, examining associations at the individual level and at the country level. Compared to those with no religious affiliation, Muslim affiliation was most strongly inversely related to suicide acceptability (B=-0.43, p<0.001), followed by Protestant (B=-0.40, p<0.001), other religious affiliation (B=-0.35, p<0.001), Catholic (B=-0.34, p<0.001), and Hindu (B=-

0.26, p<0.05); Orthodox, Buddhist, and Jewish affiliations had even weaker correlations with suicide acceptability. At the country level, however, percent Hindu in the population was the strongest predictor of negative attitudes toward suicide acceptability (B=-1.52, p<0.001) followed by percent Muslim and percent Catholic (no other affiliations were associated with suicide acceptability at the country level).

With regard to actual suicides completed, Ali and colleagues (2014) examined patterns of suicide in Malaysia using national suicide registry data for 2009 (61% Muslim, 6% Hindu). Ethnicity was examined as a possible causal factor for the 328 suicides identified. The overall suicide rate was low (1.18 per 100,000). However, Indians had the highest suicide rate of 3.67 per 100,000. This was also reflected in religious affiliation with 4.94 per 100,000 among Hindus, compared to 3.58 in Buddhists, 1.19 in Christians, 0.53 in Muslims, and 0.99 in other affiliations. Authors did not explain this finding other than say that it reflected a trend that has been observed worldwide, especially the low rate in Muslims.

In a retrospective chart review of 626 attempted suicide cases in Singapore, Mak and colleagues (2015) compared cases and protective factors against suicide across various ethnic groups (64.9% Chinese, 13.9% Malay, 15.0% Indian, 6.2% others). Indians were more likely to regard faith in religion as a protective factor compared to Chinese (44.7% vs. 24.4%, p<0.001). Indians were also more likely to have two or more protective factors compared to Chinese (OR=7.74, 95% CI 1.04-8.72). Indeed, the researchers attributed this difference to the fact that Indians place more emphasis on religion than Chinese.

Finally, Thimmaiah and colleagues (2016) compared attitudes toward suicide and suicidal behavior in a random sample of 172 Hindus and Muslims living in Bangalore, India. Attitudes toward suicide were assessed using a standard 37-item measure that explored exposure to suicidal problems and suicide. Results indicated that suicide attempt among family members (29.4% vs. 13.5%), suicidal thoughts among family members (33.8% vs. 25.9%), knowing someone with suicidal thoughts (22.0% vs. 18.3%), and knowing someone who had committed suicide (30.8% vs. 5.8%) were all significantly higher among Hindus compared to Muslims. Muslims were also more likely to disagree with a statement saying that suicide was acceptable to terminate an incurable illness, but just barely so (65.4% versus 42.7%, p<0.058).

Anxiety

Joshi and colleagues (2012) examined the relationship between religiosity, depression, and anxiety in 150 women ages 20-30 recruited from Banaras Hindu University in Varanasi, India. Religiosity was assessed with the 36-item Bhushan scale; anxiety by a standard measure assessing state, trait, and total anxiety; and depression by the 20-item CES-D. Participants were divided into high (n=83) and low (n=67) religiosity groups. State anxiety, trait anxiety, and depression were all significantly lower among those with high compared to low religiosity (all p<0.01). Likewise, when religiosity was assessed using a continuous measure, it was inversely related to state anxiety (r=-0.66), trait anxiety (r=-0.55), and depressive symptoms (r=-0.59) (all p<0.01). In a second study by this group, researchers examined the relationship between religiosity, anxiety, and pregnancy outcomes in 200 pregnant women ages 20-30 years in their third trimester of pregnancy (Kumari et al., 2013). Religiosity was again assessed by the Bhushan scale and anxiety by the state-trait anxiety scale used earlier. Results indicated that religiosity was significantly negatively correlated with anxiety and was positively correlated with healthy pregnancy outcomes.

Fuad and colleagues (2015) examined religious affiliation and mental health in 762 medical students at the International Medical School/Management and Science University in the predominantly Muslim country of Malaysia. Participants were 69.2% Muslim, 22% Hindu, 5.6% Christian, and 2.6% Buddhist. The DASS-21 was used to assess anxiety, depression, and stress. Results indicated that Hindu medical students (compared to Muslim) were at increased risk of anxiety (OR=1.56, 95% CI 1.004-2.43), but not of stress (OR=0.96, 95% CI 0.68-1.37) or depression (OR=1.09, 95% CI 0.75-1.55) (all analyses uncontrolled). Adjusting for other risk factors including life stressors, race, and year of study, Indian students (89% Hindu) remained at increased risk for anxiety (OR=2.25, 95%1.40-3.60, p=0.001). No mention of this finding was made in the discussion.

Somatic/Psychosomatic Symptoms

Grover et al (2013) examined the association between religious affiliation (77% Hindu) and explanations for somatoform disorders in 99 consecutive adult patients with the disorder (ICD-10 criteria) seen in the department of psychiatry outpatient department of a tertiary care hospital in Chandigarh, northern India. Somatoform disorders involve physical symptoms that have underlying psychological causes, where physical causes have been ruled out. Results indicated that Hindus were *less likely* than other religious groups to report explanations for illness that involved prior illness, prior treatment, family problems, marital problems, work problems, other interpersonal problems, bereavement, financial stress, bad deeds, and neglect of vows or rituals, although numbers were small providing little power for comparison. More than half of the sample attributed their symptoms to a "karma-deed-heredity" category, with 30% reporting this explanation spontaneously (third most common cause behind psychological and social causes in a list of 11 possible categories). Authors explained that this category included fate/chance, bad deeds, heredity, will of God, evil eye, sorcery, possession, neglect of vows or rituals, astrology and other supernatural causes. Furthermore, more than half (54.5%) of the sample had sought help from faith healers for current symptoms at some point in the illness. Researchers concluded that culture/religion had a significant impact on explanatory models, with more than half of patients attributing symptoms to karma and deeds. Researchers suggested that clinicians should use Hindu patients' beliefs about karma in the treatment of somatoform disorders.

Similarly, Kumar and Phookun (2015) examined the relationship between religious affiliation and somatoform disorder in 100 consecutive patients seen in the outpatient department of the department of psychiatry of Gauhati Medical College and Hospital in Assam, North-East India. Approximately half of participants were Hindu (51%) and the others were Muslim. Hindu and Muslim participants were compared on 19 symptoms and symptom clusters. No significant difference was reported on any symptoms except weakness, fatigue and anxiety. Muslims were more likely than Hindus to report weakness and fatigue (46 vs. 40, p=0.03) whereas Hindus were more likely to report somatic anxiety (39 vs. 27, p=0.02).

Several recent studies in Hindu populations have examined relationships between religious affiliation or religiosity and chronic mental disorders such as schizophrenia, obsessive-compulsive disorder, and bipolar disorder.

Schizophrenia

Recall the Shah et al (2011a) study on coping described earlier that involved 103 outpatients with schizophrenia in Chandigarh, India (73% Hindu). In a third report from that study (Shah et al., 2011b), "spirituality" (part of the WHO-QOL-100 scale) was associated with greater functional independence, better social relationships, and overall psychological health. This finding is not surprisingly since this section of the WHO-QOL-100 focused specifically on having meaning/purpose. The "faith" subscale of the WHO-QOL-SRPB measure (likewise heavily contaminated with indicators of mental health, as discussed earlier) was also associated with every dimensions of quality of life: physical, psychological, functional independence, social relationships, environment, and overall (with p<0.001 for each). Other than the earlier report by Shah et al (2011a) on coping and the Kate et al (2013) study on schizophrenia caregivers (all results coming from the same sample and research team), no other recent studies could be found that examined religious involvement and mental health among Hindu patients with schizophrenia. Thus, there is a significant research gap here that needs to be filled by future studies.

Obsessive Compulsive Disorder (OCD)

Jaisoorya and colleagues (2015) examined relationships between religious affiliation and OCD among 7,560 students enrolled at 73 schools in Ernakulam, India. OCD was assessed using a section from the Clinical Interview Schedule-Revised. Results indicated that 0.80% of students met ICD-10 criteria for OCD. Distribution of OCD by religious affiliation indicated that 23 of 3706 (0.62%) were Hindus, 20 out of 2335 were Christians (0.88%), 17 out of 1325 (1.28%) were Muslims, and 1 out of 14 were affiliated with other faith traditions (7.14%) (p=0.01). Thus, Hindu students had the lowest prevalence of OCD among all religious groups.

In a study of 201 outpatients with OCD in Calcutta, India, Das and Raychaudhuri (2016) found that those with more severe OCD (based on YBOCS scores) were more religious and more likely to be involved in religious rituals (as assessed by patients and informants during qualitative interviews). Of 43 patients from rural areas with extreme/severe OCD based on YBOCS scores, 31 (72%) were religious and practicing religious rituals, compared to only 4 (27%) of 15 patients suffering from moderate/mild OCD. Of 38 patients from semi-rural areas with extreme/severe OCD, 25 (66%) were religious, compared to only 3 (33%) of 9 patients with moderate/mild OCD.

Bipolar Disorder

In a study of 185 Indian patients with bipolar disorder (all in remission), Grover and colleagues (2016) examined level of religiosity, religious or supernatural beliefs, and religious psychopathology, along with the perceived causes of symptoms, and treatment seeking practices. Depressive and manic symptoms were assessed using standard scales (HDRS, YMRS, and GAF). More than one-third of participants (37.8%) indicated they had experienced psychopathology that included religious or supernatural content; nearly half (45.4%) believed that there was a religious or supernatural cause for their illness, the most common cause being God's will (30.8%); and nearly half (44.3%) had initially sought treatment from a religious or faith healer. While almost of these patients believed in God (90%), only 30% reported their physician had addressed religious issues in their treatment.

Substance Use/Abuse

Several studies have also examined the relationship between religious affiliation/religiosity and drinking alcoholic beverages or using other illegal/harmful substances. In a study of 509 undergraduate students at the University of the West Indies (51% Christian, 31% Hindu, 11% Muslim, 6% "other"), Dhanookdhary and colleagues (2010) found that alcohol, tobacco, and marijuana use differed significantly across religious affiliation. Alcohol was most commonly used by those with "other" religious affiliations (81%), Hindus (77%), Christians (73%), and Muslims (31%) (p<0.001); there was no significant difference in tobacco use across religious groups (30% of other affiliations, 18% of Christians, 16% of Hindus, and 13% of Muslims) (p=0.28); and marijuana was most commonly used by those with "other" religious affiliations (33%), Hindus (12%), Muslims (7%), and Christians (5%) (p=0.02). Thus, a relatively higher percentage of Hindu undergraduates use alcohol (77%); less frequent is tobacco (16%) or marijuana (12%) use. Differences from other religious groups vary by the particular substance used and the particular religious group.

Uddin (2011) examined the association between religious affiliation and arrack drinking (a form of alcohol) in rural Bangladesh.

Out of 760 male arrack drinkers, a random sample of 391 (30% Muslim, 26% Hindu, 23% Santal, 23% Oraon) was selected and assessed. Muslims make up 80% of the population in Bangladesh. While social stress was lower among Muslims and Hindus compared to the other religious/ethnic groups, social stress was a strong risk factor for continued arrack drinking in Hindus. Overall, Hindus were least likely to be involved in chronic drinking, were least likely to consume "hard" drinks, and were least likely (along with Muslims) to drink frequently.

Luczak and colleagues (2014) explored the connection between religion and alcohol use in 1,209 middle-age adults living on the island of Mauritius (an island off Madagascar in the Indian Ocean). Participants were 10% Tamil (a Hindu group), 40% Hindu, 24% Catholic, and 22% Muslim. Researchers noted that in Hinduism, moderate alcohol use is generally accepted, although heavy use is discouraged. According to Hindu beliefs, alcohol use (and other *tamasic* foods) may cause "ignorance" or "violent tendencies" and so should be avoided, especially in excess. After controlling for occupation, education, marital status, and gender, results indicated that compared to Hindus (the reference group), Muslims were least likely to "use alcohol at some point in their life" (lifetime OR=0.03, 95% CI 0.02-0.05), followed by Tamil (OR=1.56, 95% CI 0.87-2.81), and Catholic (OR=2.63, 95% CI 1.65-4.20). For current use, again Muslims were least likely compared to Hindus (OR=0.02, 95% CI 0.01-0.04), then Tamil (OR=1.45, 95% CI 0.87-2.43), and then Catholic (OR=2.01, 95% CI 1.35-2.98). Alcohol use disorder (lifetime) was also least common in Muslims compared to Hindus (OR=0.18, 95% CI 0.09-0.38), Tamil (OR=1.25, 95% CI 0.71-2.22), and Catholic (OR=1.99, 95% CI 1.31-3.00). Thus, Muslims and Hindus used the least alcohol and had less problems with alcohol (especially compared to Catholics), and also had higher levels of abstinence, resulting in lower likelihood of alcohol use disorders.

Psychological Well-being

Besides studies in Hindus on religion and mental disorders or emotional symptoms, a number of reports have examined the relationship between religious affiliation or religiosity and good mental health characterized by high psychological well-being, life satisfaction, happiness, and other positive emotions. Differences may exist in how

Hindus in India conceptualize well-being and happiness compared to how Westerners view them. For example, Joshanloo (2014) examined differences between Eastern (Hinduism, Buddhism, Taoism, Confucianism, Suffism) and Western views on happiness. He identified six fundamental differences between East and West in what is considered to be the "good life." He indicated that Eastern views of happiness emphasize eudaimonic well-being (meaning and self-realization), whereas Western views focus primarily on hedonic well-being (pleasure attainment and pain avoidance). The six fundamental differences noted between Eastern and Western views (respectively) were self-transcendence vs. self-enhancement, eudaimonism vs. hedonism, harmony vs. mastery, contentment vs. satisfaction, valuing suffering vs. avoiding it, and relevance vs. 'relative irrelevance' of spirituality/religion. Along these same lines, Nisbett and colleagues (2001) have described the differences between holistic systems of thinking in Eastern cultures compared to more analytic cognitive processes in the West. Thus, the findings below on Hinduism and well-being should be interpreted in light of these differences in perspective.

In studying the effects of **religious pilgrimage** on psychological well-being, Tewari and colleagues (2012) compared 416 pilgrims (called Kalpwasis) traveling to a holy site with a control group of 127 non-pilgrims (no information on controls except that they did not go on pilgrimage, but were comparable to pilgrims -- see below). The holy site visited is at the confluence of the Ganges and Yamuna rivers where a month-long festival (Magh Mela) is held. This festival, held every year is visited by millions of pilgrims. The 6-year festival is visited by an estimated 20 million pilgrims and the 12-year festival by more than 50 million. Pilgrims go through great hardships to get there (most often walking) and stay in squalid conditions for the month (without heat, minimal sanitary facilities, sleeping on ground, often with temperatures close to 0 centigrade). Clearly, these conditions are not physically conducive to mental or physical well-being.

The present study was not an RCT, but a longitudinal study that compared the psychological and physical well-being of pilgrims and controls. Psychological well-being and physical symptoms were assessed one month before the pilgrimage and one month afterwards (T1 and T2 separate on average by 90 days). Age (64 vs. 61), gender

(57% female vs. 50%), and case level (92% general vs. 86%) were similar between pilgrims and controls, and these differences were adjusted for in analyses. Results indicated that psychological well-being increased (group by time interaction p=0.01) and symptoms of ill-health decreased (group by time interaction p=0.04) in pilgrims compared to controls between T1 and T2.

Ganga and Kutty (2013) compared frequency of positive emotions across different religious affiliations in a random sample of 453 young persons in the age range 18-24 in Kerala, India. Religious composition of the sample was 325 Hindus, 62 Christians, and 66 Muslims. The Achutha Menon Centre Positive Mental Health Scale was used to assess positive emotions. Results indicated that Hindus and Christians scored significantly higher on the scale compared to Muslims who scored the lowest (p<0.001), especially in the domains of belief in the dignity and worth of others, productivity, and community contribution. The difference remained significant after controlling for quality of home learning environment, status in school, single vs. both parents in home, gender, and marital status.

Harding and colleagues (2015) surveyed a total of 6,643 students 11-13 years old attending schools in London boroughs (United Kingdom), of whom 4,785 were followed up when ages 14-16, and 665 when ages 21-23. The sampling scheme was to recruit 100 students in each ethnic group: White British, Indian (n=419, 59% Hindu), Pakistani or Bangladeshi, Black African, Black Caribbean, and other. The 20-item Strengths and Difficulties Questionnaire was used to assess mental health, producing a Total Difficulties Score (TDS). While the best mental health scores were found among Indian girls, the worst scores were in Indian boys. For both girls and boys as a group (all ethnicities combined), attendance at religious services was associated with better mental health at each evaluation from ages 11 to 16. Researchers attributed this finding to (1) family support from a religious community with shared values, and (2) greater parental control that is more normative in such communities where lack of autonomy is viewed by these adolescents as the norm. By ages 21-23, however, the positive associations between religious involvement and TDS scores disappeared.

Abdel-Khalek and Singh (2014) examined the relationship between religiosity and self-esteem, mental health, anxiety, and optimism/pessimism in 400 Indian university students enrolled at schools in the Uttar Pradesh Province in India (200 women and 200 men). Religiosity was assessed using two questions that asked about level of self-rated religiosity in general and self-rated religiosity in comparison to others (each rated on a 0 to 10 scale). Single questions were used to assess estimation of physical health, mental health, happiness, and satisfaction with life (all on 0 to 10 scales). Multi-item measures were used to assess self-esteem (Rosenberg), mental health, anxiety, and optimism-pessimism (using scales developed by the lead author). Results indicated that religiosity was significantly higher in women than in men. Religiosity was significantly and positively associated with mental health, happiness, and life satisfaction among men, and with satisfaction with life, self-esteem, optimism and lower anxiety in women. Regression analyses revealed a significant positive association between religiosity and life satisfaction in men, and with self-esteem, mental health, and optimism in women.

Singh (2014) surveyed 150 University students attending Banaras Hindu University in Varanasi, India, examining the relationship between religiosity, well-being, and emotional regulation. Measures included the 18-item Cognitive Emotion Regulation Questionnaire (which assesses cognitive strategies used in response to threatening or stressful life events), the 20-item Age Universal Religious Orientation Scale (which assesses intrinsic and extrinsic religiosity, dividing the sample into low, medium, and high groups), Diener's 5-item Life Satisfaction Scale, the 20-item Positive and Negative Affect Scale (PANAS), and the 29-item Oxford Happiness Questionnaire. Results (uncontrolled) indicated that high religiosity was positively associated with life satisfaction, positive affect, happiness, functional emotional regulation, overall well-being, and was negatively associated with negative affect and dysfunctional emotional regulation.

In another report by Singh (2015), the researcher examined relationships between spiritual practices and psychological well-being among 204 Hindus living in northern India recruited from temples in the region. The average age of participants was 34.4 years. Spiritual involvement was measured by the Spiritual Practices Scale-Hindus (developed by the author and a colleague) consisting of three subscales: positive transformation, self-purification, and expanding awareness. Psychological well-being was assessed using the 28-item

Psychological Well-Being Questionnaire. Not surprisingly, given the measure of spiritual involvement that included indicators of positive mental health, all three dimensions were positively associated with psychological well-being (r's ranging from 0.24-0.31, p<0.01).

International Studies on Well-being

Data on religion and well-being was collected during the three international surveys discussed in chapter 4. These surveys assessed happiness, life satisfaction, sense of purpose/meaning, and role of religion in coping. In the ISSP (2008), Hindus were significantly more likely to indicate that they were very happy compared to non-Hindus (35.6% vs. 26.4%, p<0.01) (**Table 1**). However, among Hindus, "importance of religion in life" was only weakly associated with happiness (r=0.07, p=0.31, n=199). Hindus in the WVS (2005-2006) were also more likely to say they were very happy compared to members of other religious groups (33.0% vs. 28.2%, p<0.0001), and among Hindus, religiosity was correlated with greater happiness (r=0.19, p<0.0001, n=1910) and with greater life satisfaction (r=0.20, p<0.0001, n=1879). In the GAP (2009) study, as well, Hindus were significantly more likely than non-Hindus to say they were very satisfied with life (49.0% vs. 30.2%, p<0.0001) (Table 14.2), although among Hindus, importance of religion in life was not related to happiness (r=0.01, p=0.54, n=1856).

Hindus in the ISSP study were equally as likely as non-Hindus to reject the notion that "life does not serve any purpose" (71.6% vs. 68.1%); among Hindus, religiosity was only weakly correlated with agreeing that life serves a purpose (r=0.12, p=0.08, n=197). Hindus were more likely than non-Hindus to strongly agree that religion helps people "find inner peace and happiness" (51.8% vs. 35.3%, p<0.0001) and helps people "gain comfort in times of trouble or sorrow" (52.0% vs. 39.0%, p<0.001). Not surprisingly, religiosity was strongly correlated with feeling that religion helps people to find inner peace and happiness (r=0.29, p<0.0001, n=197).

Thus, in all three cross-national studies involving random samples of the adults, Hindus scored higher on well-being, although in only one of three studies was religiosity in Hindus related to significantly greater happiness and life satisfaction.

Table 1. Comparison of well-being between Hindus, members of other religious groups, and the non-affiliated

	Hindus % (N)/Mean (SD)	Non-Hindus % (N)/Mean (SD)	No Affiliation % (N)/Mean (SD)
International Social Survey Program	100.0 (203)	100.0 (46,463)	100.0 (12,559)
Overall, how happy are you?			
Very happy	35.6 (72) *[1]	26.4 (12,046)	22.2 (2,714)***[2]
Life does not serve any purpose			
Disagree	71.6 (101) ns	68.1 (19,856)	73.5 (6,669) ***
R helps find inner peace/happiness			
Strongly agree	51.8 (103) ***	35.3 (15,384)	12.1 (1,365) ***
R helps gain comfort in sorrow			
Strongly agree	52.0 (104) **	39.0 (17,086)	17.9 (2,039) ***
Global Attitudes Project	100.0 (1,858)	100.0 (3,245)	100.0 (668)
Satisfied with life overall?			
Very satisfied	49.0 (914) ***	30.2 (978) ***	43.7 (291) ***
World Values Survey	100.0 (1,962)	100.0 (66,041)	100.0 (14,631)
Taking all things together, how happy?			
Very happy	33.0 (645) ***	28.2 (18,793) *	26.9 (3,888)***

ns not significant, i.e., $p \geq 0.01$; $*p < 0.01$; $**p < 0.001$; $***p < 0.0001$, by χ^2 for categorical Mantel-Haenszel χ^2 for ordinal, and analysis of variance for continuous outcomes
[1] applies to difference between Hindus and non-Hindus; [2] differences between all 3 groups provided for demographics and mental health. @R=religious or religion

International Social Survey Program-III (2008) surveyed a random sample of 59,063 citizens ages 15-90 from 40 countries (Australia, Austria, Belgium - Flanders, Chile, Croatia, Cyprus, Czech Republic, Denmark, Dominican Republic, Finland, France, Germany, Great Britain, Hungary, Ireland, Israel, Italy, Latvia, Mexico, Netherlands, New Zealand, Northern Ireland, Norway, Philippines, Poland, Portugal, Russia, Slovakia, Slovenia, Spain, South Africa, Sweden, Switzerland, Turkey, Ukraine, Uruguay, the United States of America, Venezuela). **Note that Hindus in this sample come primarily from South Africa (69.5%) and Great Britain (10.8%)**; non-Hindus more equally distributed across all countries. Interviews were conducted face-to-face, by telephone, and through self-completed postal questionnaires. The data downloaded from Association of Religion Data Archives, www.TheARDA.com, and were collected by Dr. Max Haller and his team at the Institut für Soziologie, Universität Graz, Austria (accessed 11/7/16).

Global Attitudes Project 2009 surveyed a random sample of 26,397 citizens ages 18 years or older from 25 countries. Information on Hindu affiliation was collected in India, Great Britain, Indonesia, Pakistan, and Canada, so survey results from these countries only were included in data presented here (**97.3% of Hindus here were from India; most non-Hindus [67.9%] from Pakistan and Indonesia**). Data were collected by telephone and face-to-face inter-views by the Princeton Survey Research Associates International, supported by the Pew Research Center as part of their 2009 Pew Global Attitudes Survey. The data were downloaded from the Association of Religion Data Archives, www.TheARDA.com. Pew Research Center bears no responsibility for analyses/ interpretations of data presented here (accessed 11/17/16).

World Values Survey 2005-2006 surveyed a random national sample of 83,879 adults ages 18-85 from more than 80 countries (approximately 1000 per country using full probability sampling). **Most Hindus in this sample were from India (77.1%) or Trinidad & Tobago (11.8%)**. Data collection was face-to-face interviewing; carried out by an international network of social scientists, with local funding for each survey. The data were downloaded from WORLD VALUES SURVEY, Wave 5, 2005-2008, OFFICIAL AGGREGATE v.20140429. World Values Survey Association [www.worldvaluessurvey.org]. Aggregate File Producer: Asep/JDS, Madrid SPAIN) retrieved from http://www.worldvaluessurvey.org/WVSDocumentationWV5.jsp (accessed 11-7-16)

In summary, of these nine studies (5 in regional and 3 in national/international samples), five (56%) found a significant correlation between religious/spiritual involvement and greater psychological well-being or positive mental health in Hindus. This is true for the effects of going on a religious pilgrimage, and for studies in adolescents, university students, and younger adults. These findings are similar to recent studies conducted in Christians and Muslims when examining religiosity and positive emotions. Five studies compared Hindus and non-Hindus on well-being, with 4 of 5 reporting higher well-being in Hindus (3 of 3 national/international studies).

Religious Interventions

A systematic review of studies examining complementary and alternative therapies directed at mental health in China and India (published in the Lancet), identified nine studies that examined the benefits of yoga in treating depression, schizophrenia, anxiety disorders, and addiction (Thirthalli et al., 2016). Of those nine studies, six were judged to have found positive results based on "low quality evidence"; one study reported negative results based on low quality evidence; and two studies reported mixed results from low quality evidence; no studies were rated as providing positive results from "high quality evidence." This is the only recent research I could find examining Hindu-based interventions.

Treatment Seeking

In a survey of 1,092 adults age 60 or over in Singapore (National Mental Survey of Elderly Singaporeans), Ng and colleagues (2011) found that older persons with any religious affiliation had a *higher prevalence* of mental health problems than those with no religious affiliation, and also less often sought help from mental healthcare professionals. The sample was comprised of 57% Buddhists/Taoists, 17% Christians, 14% Muslims, 6% Hindus, and 7% with no religious affiliation (consistent with the prevalence of Hindus in the general population estimated at 5%). The prevalence of mental disorders was highest among Muslims (17.6%), next highest in Hindus (14.9%) and Christians (14.1%), and lowest in Buddhists/Taoists (9.4%). Those with no religious affiliation had the lowest prevalence of mental disorders (7.6%). Multivariate analyses (controlling for presence of mental disorder, mental health, disability, gender, age, ethnicity, education, health beliefs, caregiver support, and financial difficulty) revealed that treatment seeking was lowest for Christians (OR=0.12, 95% CI 0.02-0.57), similar for Muslims (OR=0.12, 95% CI 0.01-1.31), next lowest for Hindus (OR=0.21, 95% CI .02-2.56), and highest for Buddhists (OR=0.59, 95% CI 0.18-1.88), and all lower than the comparison group with no religious affiliation.

Conclusions

Recent research is generally consistent with research published prior to 2010. Mental disorders are not uncommon among Hindus, but are not more common in Hindus than in non-Hindus. As noted earlier, Hindus often ascribe mental illness to religious factors and often consult traditional healers before consulting mental health professionals. In the next chapter, I summarize the research findings on religiosity and well-being in Hindus, and the findings from studies that compared the mental health of Hindus and non-Hindus.

CHAPTER 8

RESEARCH SUMMARY
AND FUTURE DIRECTIONS

In this chapter, I summarize the research findings (early research, recent research, and overall), examine methodological challenges when conducting research on religiosity and mental health in Hindus, and discuss directions for future research necessary to move the field forward.

Early Research (from Chapter 6)
Thirteen studies compared Hindus and non-Hindus (usually Muslims and Christians), with 3 studies (23%) reporting better mental health or less substance use/abuse (MH/SU) in Hindus, 5 (42%) reporting worse MH/SU in Hindus, 3 finding no difference, and 2 reporting mixed results (Hindus with better MH/SU than some and worse MH/SU than others). Thus, in this early research, Hindu religious affiliation was inconsistently related to MH/SU, depending on the particular location and study. With regard to the relationship between religiosity and MH/SU in Hindus, 17 quantitative studies examined this association (including four clinical trials). Of those, 11 (65%) reported a positive correlation between religious involvement and better MH/SU (or greater improvement in response to a Hindu-

based intervention), 2 (12%) reported worse MH/SU, 3 found no association, and 1 reported mixed findings (public religious activities related to better mental health, private religious activities related to worse). The majority of these quantitative studies, then, found that religiosity in Hindus is related to better mental health and less substance use/abuse. All four clinical trials reported that Hindu yoga-type interventions had beneficial effects on mental health.

Latest Research (from Chapter 7)
Of the 22 studies that compared Hindus and non-Hindus (including three national/cross-national studies), 9 (41%) reported better MH/SU in Hindus, 8 (36%) found worse MH/SU, and 5 reported mixed findings (better MH/SU than some, worse than others). With regard to religiosity and MH/SU in Hindus, 12 of 16 studies (75%) conducted since 2010 reported better MH/SU in those who were more religious, 2 reported worse MH/SU (13%), and 2 reported no association. These results are comparable to earlier studies, with the majority reporting less depression and anxiety, negative attitudes toward suicide and lower rates of suicide, greater self-esteem and mastery (especially in older adults), and less substance use (in Hindus vs. other religions, except Muslims). Several large studies, though, reported worse mental health and greater substance use in Hindus, more severe OCD symptoms in religious Hindus, and one study reported more mental disorder and less treatment seeking in Hindus compared to those with no religious affiliation (in Singapore). Recent intervention studies found that integrated yoga treatments for depression and other mental disorders have at least some benefit, although the evidence is largely of low quality. Finally, qualitative studies confirm (a) the importance of religion in the lives of Hindu immigrants, (b) the frequent perception of religious and supernatural beliefs as a cause for symptoms in somatoform disorder and bipolar disorder, and (c) the frequent use of faith healers to treat these conditions. When older Hindus are compared to older non-Hindus in terms of treatment seeking, Hindus are more likely than Christians or Muslims to seek treatment for mental health problems but are less likely than Buddhists or those with no religious affiliation to do so, again based on a single study conducted in Singapore.

Overall Summary

Over the past 50 years, at least 35 quantitative studies have compared Hindus and non-Hindus on MH/SU. Of those, 12 (34%) reported better MH/SU, 13 (37%) worse MH/SU, 3 found no difference between Hindus and non-Hindus, and 7 reported that Hindus had better MH/SU than some religious groups, but worse than others. With regard to religiosity, at least 33 studies have examined the relationship between religiosity and MH/SU or the effects of Hindu-based religious interventions. Of those, 23 (70%) found better MH/SU among Hindus who were more religious or receiving religious interventions, 4 (12%) reported worse MH/SU, and 6 (18%) reported no association or mixed results.

Therefore, one-third (34%) of studies report better mental health or less substance use in Hindus (vs. non-Hindus), about one-third (37%) found worse mental health or greater substance use in Hindus, and one-third (29%) reported no difference or mixed results. More importantly, over two-thirds (70%) of studies in Hindus found that greater religiosity was associated with significantly better mental health, greater well-being, or less substance use/abuse (or mental health was improved in response to Hindu-based interventions). Furthermore, the increasing suicide rate in India in recent years is concerning, and is possibly due to increased secularization in India as it becomes more westernized and technologically advanced.

However, one cannot ignore the 37% of studies that found worse MH/SU among Hindus (vs. non-Hindus). Those studies did not examine individual religiosity, which as noted above, has been associated with better mental health in the vast majority of studies. One also cannot disregard the 12% of studies that reported worse MH/SU in Hindus who were more religious. Nevertheless, note that the negative reports on religious involvement and mental health often came from studies of psychiatric patients (with religious delusions or connected with more severe OCD symptoms), adolescents or college students (probably with less than a mature religious faith), Hindus in countries where they are "outsiders" (making up only about 5% of the population such as in Malaysia or Singapore), or displaced Hindu refugees or Hindus with HIV/AIDS (where emotional distress may have caused an increase in religious involvement, not vice-versa).

Finally, analysis of three large population-based studies examining random samples of adults throughout the world found that Hindus scored higher on well-being than members of other religious groups in all three surveys, and religiosity was related to greater happiness and life satisfaction among Hindus in one of these (and a trend in that direction was also found in one of the two remaining studies). Thus, the evidence that Hindus have worse mental health than non-Hindus is inconsistent, and greater religious involvement by Hindus is clearly related to better mental health in most cases (70% of studies). Hindu beliefs and practices, then, appear to have a positive impact on coping with stress and overall mental health. Of course, this judgement is made based on the limited research now available.

Methodological Issues

Numerous methodological limitations affect both earlier and more recent studies of religious involvement/affiliation and mental health in Hindus. First, most studies are cross-sectional, forgoing any definitive conclusions with regard to causal direction of the relationships found; only a couple were prospective and followed participants over time. Second, many reports did not control for all relevant confounders that could have explained associations (such as socioeconomic status). Third, many studies involved small non-representative regional samples, limiting generalizability. Fourth, and particularly concerning, several studies used measures of religiosity that were contaminated by indicators of mental health making interpretation of the results impossible (other than concluding that good mental health is related to good mental health, i.e., which is circular and does not have any meaning). Even when measures of religiosity were not contaminated, they were often weak and poorly attuned to the religion that most Hindus practice. Finally, intervention studies (other than Yoga integrated therapies) were rare, providing little information on how Hindu religiosity itself affects mental health. Based on the systematic review of earlier studies and the selective review of more recent studies, one may conclude that research on religiosity in Hindus, while now growing, lags far behind that reported in Christian or Muslim populations.

Future Directions

Research on religion and mental health in Hindus is just beginning, and there is much work to be done to substantiate the generally positive results uncovered in this review. In particular, prospective studies are needed to assess whether religious involvement leads to better mental health outcomes over time, allowing for some speculation about the causal direction in these relationships. Of course, randomized clinical trials are needed to identify effective clinical interventions based on Hindu religious beliefs and practices that can be used in the treatment of emotional disorders or to support those with chronic mental illness (and family members caring for them). In addition, studies are needed that examine the effectiveness of co-therapy that involves mental health professionals working with traditional healers in providing care for Hindus with mental disorder. Finally, research is needed to better understand when, how, and why Hindus (and in some circumstances, even devoutly religious Hindus) experience worse mental health.

Conclusions

When Hindus are compared to non-Hindus, quantitative studies indicate that one-third have better mental health and less substance use/abuse, one-third have worse mental health, and one-third indicate similar mental health. When level of religiosity and mental health are examined within Hindu populations, 70% of studies report better mental health among the more religious. While systematic research on Hindu beliefs/practices and mental health is still in its infancy and numerous methodological problems are present in existing studies, this chapter has described the kind of future research that is needed. Hinduism is a faith tradition that for nearly 3,000 years has focused on the relief of suffering, and we need to know how Hindu beliefs and practices accomplish this (and need to identify situations in which it fails to do so and try to understand why).

CHAPTER 9

CLINICAL APPLICATIONS

What, then, does the mental health professional, pastoral counselor or Hindu clergy do with this information? I begin with a case vignette[1] to illustrate the situation that mental health professionals and even clergy may find themselves in when seeking to help Hindu clients.

Case Vignette

> Raja Gupta is a 39 year old executive at a pharmaceutical company who has come to see his mental health counselor for feelings of high stress and depressive symptoms. He reports that his job is putting too much pressure on him, and he is having trouble sleeping, lacks energy and motivation, and has been losing weight. Raja is a devout Hindu and asks his therapist whether she knows of any Hindu practices might help reduce his stress level and relieve his depressive symptoms. His therapist is

---

[1] Details of this case has been altered to protect the identity of the individual being discussed

not sure how to respond since she knows nothing about Hinduism. After asking the patient, "Have you tried yoga?" (the only Hindu practice the therapist knows about), the therapist directs the conversation to more secular issues that she feels comfortable dealing with.

The suggestions I make in this chapter are based on knowledge about Hindu beliefs and practices discussed earlier, evidence from systematic research, clinical experience with faith-based interventions, and simply common sense.

1. Take a Spiritual History

A spiritual history should always be taken on initial evaluation, or soon afterwards. The purpose of the spiritual history is to identify the specific Hindu beliefs of the client, the importance of those beliefs to the person, and the extent to which beliefs and practices are adhered to. Finally, both good and bad experiences with the Hindu faith tradition across the client's lifetime should be asked about. This information will be valuable in deciding on the treatment approach and in providing treatment that meets the minimum standard of showing respect for clients' personal beliefs and values (as required by most credentialing organizations at least in the U.S.). Mental health professionals should assume nothing in this regard, but rather have each client educate them about (a) what role their Hindu faith plays in life, (b) how that faith helps them to deal with their illness or associated life stressors, and (c) how Hindu beliefs/practices may be initiating, worsening or maintaining the illness.

If the therapist is uncomfortable asking about religious issues (i.e., taking a spiritual history) then such resistance must be overcome with training and practice. Learning about the role that religion plays in the Hindu client's illness, particularly when it influences just about everything in that person's psychological, behavioral, social, and work life (Hinduism is often described as a "way of life"), is quickly becoming the standard of care. Again, this does not mean the therapist needs to integrate those Hindu beliefs into the treatment, but knowing about them will be essential in providing therapy that is sensitive to and respectful of those beliefs.

Taking a detailed spiritual history is the most important recommendation that I can make for those treating Hindu clients.

Knowing something about the religious beliefs and practices of Hindus (as described in this book and elsewhere) will help the mental health professional make informed inquires in this regard. However, given the wide range of religious beliefs and practices among Hindus, clinicians should not assume that what they know about Hindu beliefs applies to a particular client sitting in front of them. Instead, mental health professionals and clergy should ask each person about what he or she believes and what types of religious practices are important to them (if any) in coping with their illness. In particular, it is important to understand what the client feels is the underlying cause of the illness (especially the role that "God's will" or "bad karma" may be playing).

2. Don't forget the family (and broader community)

Hindu clients will each come out of a particular family and community of friends and support persons. Unlike Westerners who treasure their independence and self-sufficiency, Hindus are often heavily dependent on relationships within the family and the community (as part of South Asian culture). Therefore, religious beliefs and religiosity of the client's family of origin, and the religious beliefs and religiosity of the client's support system need to be inquired about as well. This will give the clinician a sense of whether changes made during therapy will be supported (or opposed) after the client leaves the therapist's office. Although patient confidentiality should be maintained at all times, and most clinical encounters will involve only the client and the treating professional, there will be times when the therapist will need to ask permission from the patient to include the family during the assessment and the treatment.

3. Provide a Safe Place

Provide an open and safe place where clients can talk freely about their religion, good or bad, without judgment. Maintain a respectful, interested, and receptive attitude at all times with regard to the client's Hindu beliefs and practices (whether the person is currently active in their faith tradition or not, whether he or she speaks well of their faith or not).

4. **Be Supportive and Neutral**
Be respectful and supportive of the Hindu client's religious beliefs/practices that he or she finds helpful (or might find helpful in the future) as a way of coping with emotional issues. However, always do so from the client's perspective. If the client is receptive and open to healthy religious practices, and these beliefs/practices are not clearly pathological, then they may be encouraged. If the client shows any resistance, don't push; however, it may be informative to gently explore where the resistance to religious beliefs/practices is coming from in a future session. Never give clients the impression that they are not religious enough, since they probably get plenty of that from family members or those in their religious community. Whether you are a psychiatrist prescribing biological therapies or a therapist providing counseling, the mental health professional should be viewed by the client as neutral, interested in, open to and supportive of the client's Hindu faith tradition, but always on the client's side and never judgmental. This advice also applies to Hindu clergy who may be counseling members of their temple or religious community.

5. **Accommodate the Environment**
In office or hospital settings, every effort should be made to accommodate the environment to make it easier for Hindu patients to practice their religion. This may include placing a copy of the Bhagavad Gita or of The Hindu magazine on a table in the waiting room. In the hospital, this may include accommodating the chapel so that Hindu patients feel comfortable worshiping in this setting.

6. **Experience with Traditional Healers**
Given the frequent use of traditional or faith healers by Hindus in East Asia (as well as by Hindu immigrants to other countries in the West), clinicians should ask about what other sources of help outside the mainstream mental health profession that Hindu patients have sought. Family members may be a particularly important source of such information.

7. **Consider a Religiously-Integrated Therapy**
If clients prefer this approach and therapists are willing and qualified, religiously-integrated cognitive behavioral therapy (CBT) from a

Hindu perspective should be considered for those with emotional disorders. There are resources that may help the therapist or Hindu clergy in this regard. This includes a Hindu CBT manual, along with therapist and patient workbooks, and an introductory video, that can be accessed at the Center for Spirituality, Theology and Health website, all without charge (CSTH, 2014). Religiously-integrated CBT, including that from a Hindu perspective, is an evidence-based treatment that has documented effectiveness in the treatment for depression, especially in highly religious patients (Koenig et al., 2015).

There are also evidence-based Hindu treatments such as Omkar meditation, Hartha yoga, other integrated yoga interventions (relying on Patanjali yoga sutras and Mandukaya Karika scriptures) that have been shown to be effective in relieving a variety of emotional disorders (see Religious Interventions in Chapter 6). Another invaluable resource for self-care among Hindus is the Bhagavad Gita, which is full of wisdom on how to maintain and enhance mental health (for an easily accessible English version of the Gita, see Johnson, 1994).

8. Utilize Religious Resources

If the client is religious, but not a candidate for a religiously-integrated psychotherapy, meditation or yoga therapies, or does not prefer these approach, then the therapist should provide secular psychotherapy that is supportive and respectful of the client's Hindu beliefs. There may be times during secular psychotherapy when the client's religious beliefs may be utilized to support changes in attitude and behavior. Knowing about those religious beliefs/practices (as covered in earlier chapters) will be helpful, as will a detailed spiritual history to identify ones are particularly important to the Hindu client being treated. Consultation with knowledgeable experts in Hinduism may need to be sought as well, particularly if beliefs are to be challenged.

9. Challenge/Re-Educate

If the client's Hindu beliefs or practices are contributing to their psychopathology, and this is confirmed following consultation with an expert from the client's local Hindu congregation (after the client provides consent), then the following approach is suggested. First and foremost, the mental health professional should inquire further about the role that particular religious beliefs are playing in supporting psychopathology. The therapist should listen respectfully, gathering as much information as possible about the natural history of how religion became intertwined with the emotional problem. This must be done in an open and receptive manner and without confrontation (at least initially during this information gathering stage). There will come a time, once the therapeutic relationship is firmly established and the client feels safe and accepted, when gradual, gentle, and persistent "Socratic questioning" may help to guide the client towards a "healthier" use of their Hindu beliefs/practices. I emphasize *gradual, gentle, and persistent questioning* by an informed therapist within an atmosphere that is safe and comfortable. Arguments over religious beliefs will almost always be unsuccessful and will adversely affect the therapeutic alliance.

10. Non-Religious Hindus
If the client was raised in a Hindu family but is not actively religious, then the mental health professional should proceed with secular psychotherapy that is respectful of the client's personal and cultural beliefs. Aggressive attempts to reconnect the person to his/her Hindu faith tradition should be avoided. If the client was once religious and has now become socially isolated or is despairing for lack of meaning in life, the therapist might gently ask if the client has considered re-establishing connections with a local faith community. The therapist may help the client weigh the pluses and minuses of such re-involvement, but again always from the client's perspective and following the client's lead.

11. Consult or Refer
If addressing religion or integrating it into the treatment seems indicated in a Hindu client, and the therapist lacks the desire or experience to do so, consideration should be given to consultation with, co-therapy with, or referral to a Hindu chaplain[1] or pastoral counselor.[2] If clergy trained to provide counseling from a Hindu perspective are not available, then the therapist should consider obtaining additional training in this regard (see CSTH, 2014).

---

[1] Hindu Chaplaincy. See http://www.hinduchaplaincy.com/service.html
[2] American Association of Pastoral Counselors. See
http://aapc.org/Default.aspx?ssid=74&NavPTypeId=1708

CHAPTER 10

CONCLUSIONS

Despite widespread differences in Hindu belief and practice, the methodological limitations noted in the research described above, and the need for more systematic research, a number of tentative conclusions can be made about the relationship between Hinduism and mental health.

Hinduism is one of the oldest religions in the world (if not the oldest), and has persisted for millennia as a source of wisdom for dealing with trauma, threats to survival, unwanted change, fears surrounding death and dying, and other existential concerns. The core religious beliefs and practices of this faith tradition seek to make sense of the limitations of the human condition and to relieve the emotional and physical suffering that accompanies it. Systematic quantitative research in the majority of studies (70%) has found positive relationships between Hindu religious beliefs/practices and better psychological coping, fewer symptoms of anxiety and stress, better outcomes in severe mental disorder (Hindu temple study), increased mastery and self-esteem, and greater psychological well-being, not to mention a number of clinical trials demonstrating positive effects of Hindu practices on emotional symptoms. Sensing the benefits of these practices, Hindu patients and their families often obtain help from traditional or faith healers before seeking modern mental health care.

There is every reason, then, for clinicians to conduct a thorough assessment of Hindu beliefs and practices, learn how these are helping or hindering efforts toward recovery, and provide treatment that is sensitive to and supportive of the client's Hindu faith tradition (which may sometimes involve working with traditional healers or clergy). A barrier to integrating Hindu beliefs and practices into therapy, though, is the lack of an evidence base from systematic research to guide such efforts. However, there is enough of an evidence base now for clinicians to at least take a few sensible steps (as discussed here) to begin that integration.

REFERENCES

Abdel-Khalek, A. M., & Singh, A. P. (2014). Religiosity, subjective well-being, and anxiety in a sample of Indian university students. *Arab Journal of Psychiatry 25*(2), 201-207.

Adamczyk, A., & Hayes, B. E. (2012). Religion and sexual behaviors understanding the influence of Islamic cultures and religious affiliation for explaining sex outside of marriage. *American Sociological Review, 77*(5), 723-746.

Adler M (2012). To some Hindus, modern yoga has lost its way. *National Public Radio* (NPR), April 11 Retrieved from. http://www.npr.org/2012/04/11/150352063/to-some-hindus-modern-yoga-has-lost-its-way (accessed on 8/13/16)

Agrawal, J., Murthy, P., Philip, M., Mehrotra, S., Thennarasu, K., John, J. P., Girish N, Thippeswamy V, & Isaac, M. (2011). Socio-demographic correlates of subjective well-being in urban India. *Social Indicators Research, 101*(3), 419-434.

Akhtar, S. (1988). Four culture-bound psychiatric syndromes in India. *International Journal of Social Psychiatry, 34*(1), 70-74.

Ali, N. H., Zainun, K. A., Bahar, N., Haniff, J., Hamid, A. M., Bujang, M. A. H., & Mahmood, M. S. (2014). Pattern of suicides in 2009: data from the National Suicide Registry Malaysia. *Asia-Pacific Psychiatry, 6*(2), 217-225.

Anjana, R., & Raju, S. (2003). Management of maladjustment: A study on reciters and non-reciters of the Bhagavad Gita. *Journal of Indian Psychology, 21*(1), 21-27

Baspure, S., Jagannathan, A., Kumar, S., Varambally, S., Thirthalli, J., Venkatasubramanain, G., Nagendra, H. R., Gangadhar, B. N. (2012). Barriers to yoga therapy as an add-on treatment for schizophrenia in India. *International Journal of Yoga, 5*(1), 70-73.

Basu M (2017). 9 myths about Hinduism, debunked. *Cable Network News* (CNN), March 3. Retrieved from http://www.cnn.com/2017/03/03/world/believer-hinduism-nine-myths-debunked/ (accessed on 3/18/17)

BBC (2003). Hindu beliefs. *British Broadcasting Corporation.* Retrieved from http://www.bbc.co.uk/religion/religions/hinduism/beliefs/intro_1.shtml (accessed on 7/26/16)

Benson, G. O., Sun, F., Hodge, D. R., & Androff, D. K. (2012). Religious coping and acculturation stress among Hindu Bhutanese: A study of newly-resettled refugees in the United States. *International Social Work, 55*(4), 538-553.

Bhugra, D., Bhui, K., & Gupta, K. (2000). Bulimic disorders and sociocentric values in north India. *Social Psychiatry and Psychiatric Epidemiology, 35*(2), 86-93.

Bhushan, L. I. (1970). Religiosity scale. *Indian Journal of Psychology 45*:335-342.

Boyd, K. A., & Chung, H. (2012). Opinions toward suicide: Cross-national evaluation of cultural and religious effects on individuals. *Social Science Research, 41*(6), 1565-1580.

Bradby, H., Williams, R. (2006). Is religion or culture the key feature in changes in substance use after leaving school? Young Punjabis and a comparison group in Glasgow. *Ethnicity & Health, 11*(3), 307-324.

Castillo, R. J. (1990). Depersonalization and meditation. *Psychiatry, 53*(2), 158-168.

CSTH (2014). *Religious Cognitive Behavioral Therapy (Hindu version). 10-Session Treatment Manual for Depression in Clients with Chronic Physical Illness* (by Ciarrocchi JW, Schechter D, Pearce MJ, Koenig HG, Juthani N). Durham, NC, USA: Duke University. Retrieved from http://www.spiritualityandhealth.duke.edu/index.php/religious-cbt-study/therapy-manuals (accessed on 12/31/16)

Chattha R, Raghuram N, Venkatram P, Hongasandra NR. (2008). Treating the climacteric symptoms in Indian women with an integrated approach to yoga therapy: a randomized control study. *Menopause*, 15(5):862-70

Chaturvedi, H., Phukan, R., & Mahanta, J. (2003). The association of selected sociodemographic factors and differences in patterns of substance use: A pilot study in selected areas of Northeast India. *Substance Use & Misuse, 38*(9), 1305-1322.

Chaturvedi, S.K., & Bhandari, S. (1989). Somatization and illness behavior. *Journal of Psychosomatic Research*, 33, 147-153

Chokkanathan, S. (2013). Religiosity and well-being of older adults in Chennai, India. *Aging & Mental Health, 17*(7), 880-887.

Cramer H, Ward L, Steel A, Lauche R, Dobos G, Zhang Y (2016). Prevalence, patterns, and predictors of yoga use: Results of a U.S. nationally representative survey. *American Journal of Preventative Medicine* 50(2):230-235

Crowley N, Jenkinson G (2009). Pathological spirituality, chapter 13. In Cook C, Powell A, Simms A (eds), *Spirituality and Psychiatry*. London: Royal College of Psychiatrists Publications, pp 254-272

Dalal, A.K., & Pande, N. (1988). Psychological recovery of accident victims with temporary and permanent disability. *International Journal of Psychology*, 23, 25-40

Das, R., & Raychaudhuri, S. (2016). Disease Severity and Social Adjustment of Patients with Obsessive Compulsive Disorder from West Bengal. *International Journal of Indian Psychology* 3 (4): 81-88

De Figueiredo, J.M., & Lemkau, P.V. (1978). The prevalence of psychosomatic symptoms in a rapidly changing bilingual culture: An exploratory study. *Social Psychiatry*, 13, 125-133.

Dhanookdhary, A. M., Gomez, A. M., Khan, R., Lall, A., Murray, D., Prabhu, D., ... & Youssef, F. F. (2010). Substance use among university students at the St Augustine Campus of The University of the West Indies. *West Indian Medical Journal, 59*(6), 641-649.

Dhavamony M (2002). *Hindu-Christian Dialogue: Theological Soundings and Perspectives.* Amsterdam, Netherlands: Rodopi Bv Editions

Dhawan, N., & Sripat, K. (1986). Fear of death and religiosity as related to need for affiliation. *Psychological Studies*, 31, 35-38.

Diwan, S., Jonnalagadda, S. S., & Balaswamy, S. (2004). Resources predicting positive and negative affect during the experience of stress: a study of older Asian Indian immigrants in the United States. *Gerontologist, 44*(5), 605-614.

Doniger, W. (2015). Bhagavad-Gita. *Encyclopaedia Britannica* (online verison). Retrieved from https://www.britannica.com/topic/Bhagavadgita (accessed on 7/26/16)

Dube, K.C., Jain, S.C., Basu, A.K., & Kumar, N. (1975). Patterns of the drug habit (cannabis) in hospitalized psychiatric patients. *Bulletin on Narcotics*, 27 (2), 1-10.

Edwardraj, S., Mumtaj, K., Prasad, J. H., Kuruvilla, A., & Jacob, K. S. (2010). Perceptions about intellectual disability: a qualitative study from Vellore, South India. *Journal of Intellectual Disability Research, 54*(8), 736-748.

Flood GD (2009a). History of Hinduism. *British Broadcasting Corporation (BBC)*, August 24. Retrieved from http://www.bbc.co.uk/religion/religions/hinduism/history/history_1.shtml (accessed on 7/26/16)

Flood GD (2009b). Hindu concepts. *British Broadcasting Corporation (BBC)*, August 24. Retrieved from http://www.bbc.co.uk/religion/religions/hinduism/concepts/concepts_1.shtml (accessed on 7/26/16)

Flood GD (1996). *An Introduction to Hinduism*. Cambridge, UK: Cambridge University Press

Francis, L. J., Santosh, Y. R., Robbins, M., & Vij, S. (2008). Assessing attitude toward Hinduism: The Santosh–Francis Scale. *Mental Health, Religion and Culture, 11*(6), 609-621.

Freed, R. S., & Freed, S. A. (1990). Ghost illness in a North Indian village. *Social Science & Medicine, 30*(5), 617-623.

Fuad, M. D., Al-Zurfi, B. M. N., Abdelqader, M. A., Abu Bakar, M. F., Elnajeh, M., & Abdullah, M. R. (2015). Prevalence and risk factors of stress, anxiety and depression among medical students of a private medical university in Malaysia. *Education in Medicine Journal, 7*(2):e52-e59.

Gandhi MK (1926). *Young India* (a weekly journal written and published by Gandhi from 1919 to 1932), January 12 (no page number)

Ganga, N. S., & Kutty, V. R. (2013). Influence of religion, religiosity and spirituality on positive mental health of young people. *Mental Health, Religion & Culture, 16*(4), 435-443.

GAP (2009). Global Attitudes Project, 2009. Data were collected by telephone and face-to-face interviews by the Princeton Survey Research Associates International, supported by the Pew Research Center as part of their 2009 Pew Global Attitudes Survey. The data were downloaded from the Association of Religion Data Archives. Retrieved from http://www.thearda.com/Archive/browse.asp (accessed on 11/17/16).

Grover, S., Aneja, J., Sharma, A., Malhotra, R., Varma, S., Basu, D., & Avasthi, A. (2013). Explanatory models of somatoform disorder patients attending a psychiatry outpatient clinic: A study from North India. *International Journal of Social Psychiatry* 60 (5):492-498

Grover, S., Hazari, N., Aneja, J., Chakrabarti, S., & Avasthi, A. (2016). Influence of religion and supernatural beliefs on clinical manifestation and treatment practices in patients with bipolar disorder. *Nordic Journal of Psychiatry* 70(6):442-9

Guglani, S., Coleman, P. G., & Sonuga-Barke, E. J. (2000). Mental health of elderly Asians in Britain: a comparison of Hindus from nuclear and extended families of differing cultural identities. *International Journal of Geriatric Psychiatry, 15*(11), 1046-1053.

Gupta, S., Avasthi, A., & Kumar, S. (2011). Relationship between religiosity and psychopathology in patients with depression. *Indian Journal of Psychiatry, 53*(4), 330-335.

Gupta, V. B. (2011). How Hindus cope with disability. *Journal of Religion, Disability & Health, 15*(1), 72-78.

Gururaj G, Isaac M, Subhakrishna DK, Ranjani R (2004). Risk factors for completed suicides: A case-control study from Bangalore, India. *Injury Control & Safety Promotion* 11:183-191

Harding, S., Read, U.M., Molaodi, O.R., Cassidy, A., Maynard, M.J., Lenguerrand, E., Astell-Burt, T., Teyhan, A., Whitrow, M. and Enayat, Z.E. (2015). The Determinants of young Adult Social well-being and Health (DASH) study: diversity, psychosocial determinants and health. *Social Psychiatry and Psychiatric Epidemiology, 50*(8), pp.1173-1188.

Harinath, K., Malhotra, A. S., Pal, K., Prasad, R., Kumar, R., Kain, T. C., et al. (2004). Effects of Hatha yoga and Omkar meditation on cardiorespiratory performance, psychologic profile, and melatonin secretion. *Journal of Alternative and Complementary Medicine, 10*(2), 261-268

Hassan, M.K., & Khalique, A. (1981). Religiosity and its correlates in college students. *Journal of Psychological Researches* 25 (3): 129-136.

ISSP (2008). *International Social Survey Program*, 2008. Dataset downloaded from the Association of Religion Data Archives, and were collected by Dr. Max Haller and his team at the Institut für Soziologie, Universität Graz, Austria. Retrieved from http://www.thearda.com/Archive/browse.asp (accessed on 11/17/16).

Jain, N., Gautam, S., Jain, S., Gupta, I. D., Batra, L., Sharma, R., & Singh, H. (2012). Pathway to psychiatric care in a tertiary mental health facility in Jaipur, India. *Asian Journal of Psychiatry*, *5*(4), 303-308.

Jaisoorya, T. S., Reddy, Y. J., Thennarasu, K., Beena, K. V., Beena, M., & Jose, D. C. (2015). An epidemological study of obsessive compulsive disorder in adolescents from India. *Comprehensive Psychiatry*, *61*, 106-114.

John, A. (2012). Stress among mothers of children with intellectual disabilities in urban India: role of gender and maternal coping. *Journal of Applied Research in Intellectual Disabilities*, *25*(4), 372-382.

Johnson WJ (1994). *The Bhagavad Gita* (reissued in 2008 as part of Oxford World Classics series). NY, NY: Oxford University Press

Joshanloo, M. (2014). Eastern conceptualizations of happiness: Fundamental differences with western views. *Journal of Happiness Studies*, *15*(2), 475-493.

Joshi, S., Kumari, S., & Jain, M. (2012). Religiosity as related to women's health. *Delhi Psychiatry Journal* 15 (1):136-142

Kalokhe, A. S., Potdar, R. R., Stephenson, R., Dunkle, K. L., Paranjape, A., del Rio, C., & Sahay, S. (2015). How well does the World Health Organization definition of domestic violence work for India? *PloS One*, *10*(3), e0120909.

Kamal, Z., & Lowenthal, K. M. (2002). Suicide beliefs and behaviour among young Muslims and Hindus in the UK. *Mental Health, Religion & Culture*, *5*(2), 111-118.

Kamble, S. V., Watson, P. J., Marigoudar, S., & Chen, Z. (2014). Attitude towards Hinduism, religious orientations, and psychological adjustment in India. *Mental Health, Religion & Culture, 17*(2), 161-172.

Kate, N., Grover, S., Kulhara, P., & Nehra, R. (2013). Positive aspects of caregiving and its correlates in caregivers of schizophrenia: a study from north India. *East Asian Archives of Psychiatry, 23*(2):45-55.

Khan, S. S., Hopkins, N., Tewari, S., Srinivasan, N., Reicher, S. D., & Ozakinci, G. (2014). Efficacy and well-being in rural north India: The role of social identification with a large-scale community identity. *European Journal of Social Psychology, 44*(7), 787-798.

Knapp S (2016). God is both personal (Bhagavan) and impersonal (Brahman). http://www.stephen-knapp.com/god_is_both_%20personal_(Bhagavan)_and_impersonal_(Brahman).htm (accessed 8/12/16)

Koenig HG (2017). Unpublished report. Based on analysis of data downloaded from the ARDA Archive that contains the 2008 International Social Survey Program, 2009 Global Attitudes Project, and the 2005-2006 World Values Survey. Retrieved from: http://www.thearda.com/archive/browse.asp (last accessed 12/9/16).

Koenig HG, King DE, Carson VB (2012). *Handbook of Religion and Health*, 2nd ed. NY, NY: Oxford University Press

Koenig HG, McCullough ME, Larson DB (2001). *Handbook of Religion and Health*, 1st ed. NY, NY: Oxford University Press

Koenig HG, Pearce MJ, Nelson B, Shaw SF, Robins CJ, Daher N, Cohen HJ, Berk LS, Belinger D, Pargament KI, Rosmarin DH, Vasegh S, Kristeller J, Juthani N, Nies D, King MB (2015). Religious vs. conventional cognitive-behavioral therapy for major depression in persons with chronic medical illness. *Journal of Nervous and Mental Disease* 203(4): 243-251

Kuijpers, H. J. H., Van der Heijden, F. M. M. A., Tuinier, S., & Verhoeven, W. M. A. (2007). Meditation-induced psychosis. *Psychopathology*, *40*(6), 461-464.

Kulhara, P., Avasthi A., Sharma A. (2000) Magico-religious beliefs in schizophrenia: A study from North India. *Psychopathology* 33(2): 62–68.

Kumar, A., & Phookun, H. R (2015). Somatoform disorder: A link between psychiatry and medical symptoms with demographic profile. *ASSAM Journal of Internal Medicine* 5(2):9-15

Kumari, S., Joshi, S., & Jain, M. (2013). Religiosity, Anxiety and Pregnancy Outcomes in Indian Women. *Journal of the Indian Academy of Applied Psychology*, *39*(1), 110-116.

Luczak, S. E., Prescott, C. A., Dalais, C., Raine, A., Venables, P. H., & Mednick, S. A. (2014). Religious factors associated with alcohol involvement: Results from the Mauritian Joint Child Health Project. *Drug and Alcohol Dependence*, *135*, 37-44.

Mak, K. K., Ho, C. S., Chua, V., & Ho, R. C. (2015). Ethnic differences in suicide behavior in Singapore. *Transcultural Psychiatry*, *52*(1), 3-17.

Manoranjitham S, Charles H, Saravana B, Jayakaran R, Abraham S, Jacob KS (2007). Perceptions about suicide: a qualitative study from southern India. *National Medical Journal of India* 20: 176-179

Manoranjitham, S. D., Rajkumar, A. P., Thangadurai, P., Prasad, J., Jayakaran, R., & Jacob, K. S. (2010). Risk factors for suicide in rural south India. *The British Journal of Psychiatry*, *196*(1), 26-30.

Mishra V (1994). *The Gothic Sublime*. Albany, NY: SUNY Press, p. 249

Mohan, D., Sharma, K., & Sundaram, R. (1979). Patterns and prevalence of opium use in rural Punjab (India). *Bulletin on Narcotics*, 31, 45-56.

Mohan, K., Prasad, S. V., & Rao, P. (2004). Effects of spiritually based lifestyle change programme on well-being. *Journal of Indian Psychology 22*(1): 6-13.

Monier-Williams M (1877). *Hinduism*. London: Society for Promoting Christian Knowledge

Narayanan V (2016). Hinduism. *Encyclopedia Britannica*. Retrieved from https://www.britannica.com/topic/Hinduism (accessed on 8/11/16)

Nath, K., Bhattacharya, A., Sinha, P., & Praharaj, S. K. (2015). Devaki Syndrome: A culture-bound psychological reaction in Indian Hindu women in response to repeated pregnancy loss? *Asian Journal of Psychiatry*, 13, 13-15.

Nayak HK, Batra Sonia B, Kapoor R, Gadhavi R, Solanki A, Vyas S, Tiwari H (2011). Prevalence and pattern of stress relaxation practices in Ahmedabad city: A cross-sectional study. *IJOY International Journal of Yoga* 4(2):87-92

Ng, T. P., Nyunt, M. S. Z., Chiam, P. C., & Kua, E. H. (2011). Religion, health beliefs and the use of mental health services by the elderly. *Aging & Mental Health*, *15*(2), 143-149.

Nisbett, R. E., Peng, K., Choi, I., Norenzayan. A. (2001). Culture and systems of thought: holistic versus analytic cognition. *Psychological Review* 108 (2):291-310.

Olivelle P (1996). *Upanisads* (translated from the original Sanskrit; Oxford World's Classics). Oxford, UK: Oxford University Press

Olivelle P (2016). Upanishad. *Encyclopedia Britannica*. Retrieved from https://www.britannica.com/topic/Upanishad (accessed on 8/12/16)

Oppenheimer JR (1963). Response when asked to list the ten books that "did most to shape your vocational attitude and your philosophy of life." *Christian Century Magazine*, May 15, p. 647

Pandey, R.E. (1968). The suicide problem in India. *International Journal of Social Psychiatry*, 14, 193-200.

Patel, V., Weiss, H. A., Kirkwood, B. R., Pednekar, S., Nevrekar, P., Gupte, S., et al. (2006). Common genital complaints in women: The contribution of psychosocial and infectious factors in a population-based cohort study in Goa, India. *International Journal of Epidemiology*, *35*(6), 1478-1485.

Pew Research Center (2015). The future of world religions: Population growth projections, 2010-2050. *Religion & Public Life*, April 2. Retrieved from http://www.pewforum.org/2015/04/02/religious-projections-2010-2050 (accessed on 1/30/2017)

Prakash, O., Kar, S. K., & Rao, T. S. (2014). Indian story on semen loss and related Dhat syndrome. *Indian Journal of Psychiatry*, *56*(4), 377-382.

Prothero S (2010). *God Is Not One: The Eight Rival Religions that Run the World and Why their Differences Matter.* New York, NY: HarperOne, p. 144

Puri, M., Tamang, J., & Shah, I. (2011). Suffering in silence: consequences of sexual violence within marriage among young women in Nepal. *BMC Public Health*, *11*(1):29 (DOI: 10.1186/1471-2458-11-29)

Quack, J.F. (2012). Ignorance and utilization: mental health care outside the purview of the Indian state. *Anthropology & Medicine* 19 (3): 277-290

Raguram, R., Venkateswaran, A., Ramakrishna, J., & Weiss, M. G. (2002). Traditional community resources for mental health: A report of temple healing from India. *British Medical Journal*, *325*(7354), 38-40.

Rai, P., & Verma, B. L. (2015). A study on depression in people living with HIV/AIDS in South-West part of Uttar Pradesh, India. *South East Asia Journal of Public Health*, *5*(1), 12-17.

Rammohan, A., Rao, K., & Subbakrishna, D. (2002). Religious coping and psychological wellbeing in carers of relatives with schizophrenia. *Acta Psychiatrica Scandinavica, 105*(5), 356-362

Rollocks, S., Dass, N. (2007). Influence of religious affiliation in alcohol use among adolescents in Trinidad, Tobago, and St. Lucia: a follow-up study. *American Journal of Drug & Alcohol Abuse, 33*(1), 185-189.

Roy S (2010). Yoga: A positively un-Indian experience. *National Public Radio*, December 29. Retrieved from http://www.npr.org/2010/12/29/132207910/yoga-a-positively-un-indian-experience (last accessed 8/13/16).

Satyapriya M, Nagendra HR, Nagarathna R, Padmalatha V (2009). Effect of integrated yoga on stress and heart rate variability in pregnant women. *International Journal of Gynecology and Obstetrics* 104, 218-222.

Sax, W. (2014). Ritual healing and mental health in India. *Transcultural Psychiatry, 51*(6), 829-849.

Shah, R., Kulhara, P., Grover, S., Kumar, S., Malhotra, R., & Tyagi, S. (2011a). Relationship between spirituality/religiousness and coping in patients with residual schizophrenia. *Quality of Life Research, 20*(7), 1053-1060.

Shah, R., Kulhara, P., Grover, S., Kumar, S., Malhotra, R., & Tyagi, S. (2011b). Contribution of spirituality to quality of life in patients with residual schizophrenia. *Psychiatry Research, 190*(2), 200-205.
Sharma, I., Pandit, B., Pathak, A., & Sharma, R. (2013). Hinduism, marriage and mental illness. *Indian Journal of Psychiatry, 55*(Suppl 2), S243.

Sidhartha, T., Jena, S. (2006). Suicidal behaviors in adolescents. *Indian Journal of Pediatrics, 73*(9), 783-788

Singh, S (2014). Well-being and emotion regulation in emerging adults: The role of religiosity. *Indian Journal of Positive Psychology* 5(1): 46-50.

Singh, R. (2015). Relationship between spiritual practices and psychological well-being among Hindus. *International Journal of Indian Psychology* 3(1):104-110

Sisask, M., Värnik, A., Kolves, K., Bertolote, J. M., Bolhari, J., Botega, N. J., ... & Wasserman, D. (2010). Is religiosity a protective factor against attempted suicide: a cross-cultural case-control study. *Archives of Suicide Research, 14*(1), 44-55.

Stack, S., & Kposowa, A. J. (2011). Religion and suicide acceptability: A cross-national analysis. *Journal for the Scientific Study of Religion, 50*(2), 289-306.

Tarakeshwar, N., Pargament, K. I., & Mahoney, A. (2003). Initial development of a measure of religious coping among Hindus. *Journal of Community Psychology,* 31(6), 607-628.

Tewari, S., Khan, S., Hopkins, N., Srinivasan, N., & Reicher, S. (2012). Participation in mass gatherings can benefit well-being: Longitudinal and control data from a North Indian Hindu pilgrimage event. *PLoS One, 7*(10), e47291.

Thara, R., & Eaton, W. W. (1996). Outcome of schizophrenia: the Madras longitudinal study. *Australian and New Zealand Journal of Psychiatry,* 30(4), 516-522.

Thimmaiah, R., Poreddi, V., Ramu, R., Selvi, S., & Math, S. B. (2016). Influence of religion on attitude towards suicide: An Indian perspective. *Journal of Religion and Health* 55(6):2039-52.

Thirthalli, J., Zhou, L., Kumar, K., Gao, J., Vaid, H., Liu, H., ... & Nichter, M. (2016). Traditional, complementary, and alternative medicine approaches to mental health care and psychological wellbeing in India and China. *Lancet Psychiatry* 3(7): 660–672

Thombre, A., Sherman, A. C., & Simonton, S. (2010). Religious coping and posttraumatic growth among family caregivers of cancer patients in India. *Journal of Psychosocial Oncology, 28*(2), 173-188.

Tummala-Narra, P., Sathasivam-Rueckert, N., & Sundaram, S. (2013). Voices of older Asian Indian immigrants: Mental health implications. *Professional Psychology: Research and Practice, 44*(1), 1-10.

Uddin, E. (2011). Relationship between social stress and arrack drinking pattern: A cross-cultural comparison among Muslim, Hindu, Santal and Oraon arrack drinkers in Rasulpur of Bangladesh. *International Journal of Sociology and Social Policy, 31*(5/6), 361-388.

Varnik P (2012). Suicide in the world. *International Journal of E nvironmental Research in Public Health* 9(3):760-771.

Verghese A, John JK, Rajkumar S, Richard J, Sethi BB, Trivedi JK (1989). Factors associated with the course and outcome of schizophrenia in India: Results of a two-year multicentre follow-up study. *British Journal of Psychiatry* 154:499-503

Violatti , C. (2013). Bhagavad-Gita. *Ancient History Encyclopedia.* Retrieved from http://www.ancient.eu/Bhagavad_Gita/ (accessed on 7/26/16)

Waelde, L. C. (2004). Dissociation and meditation. *Journal of Trauma & Dissociation,* 5(2), 147-162

WHO (2014). India has highest number of suicides in the world: WHO. *The Times of India,* September 4. Retrieved from http://timesofindia.indiatimes.com/india/India-has-highest-number-of-suicides-in-the-world-WHO/articleshow/41708567.cms and from http://apps.who.int/gho/data/node.main.MHSUICIDE?lang=en (last accessed on 9-4-16)

Williams, P., Tribe, A., Wynne, A. (2012). *Buddhist Thought: A Complete Introduction to the Indian Tradition* (2nd ed). NY, NY: Routledge

WVS (2005-2006). *World Values Survey*, 2005-2006. Dataset was downloaded from the World Values Survey (WORLD VALUES SURVEY Wave 5 2005-2008 OFFICIAL AGGREGATE v.20140429. World Values Survey Association [www.worldvaluessurvey.org]. Aggregate File Producer: Asep/JDS, Madrid SPAIN). Retrieved from http://www.worldvaluessurvey.org/WVSDocumentationWV5.jsp (accessed on 11-7-16)

ABOUT THE AUTHOR

Harold G. Koenig, M.D., M.H.Sc., completed his undergraduate education at Stanford University, nursing school at San Joaquin Delta College, medical school training at the University of California at San Francisco, and geriatric medicine, psychiatry, and biostatistics training at Duke University Medical Center. He is currently board certified in general psychiatry, and formerly boarded in family medicine, geriatric medicine, and geriatric psychiatry, and is on the faculty at Duke as Professor of Psychiatry and Behavioral Sciences, and Associate Professor of Medicine. He is also Adjunct Professor in the Department of Medicine at King Abdulaziz University, Jeddah, Saudi Arabia, and in the School of Public Health at Ningxia Medical University, Yinchuan, People's Republic of China. Dr. Koenig is Director of the Center for Spirituality, Theology and Health at Duke University Medical Center, and has published extensively in the fields of mental health, geriatrics, and religion, with over 500 scientific peer-reviewed articles and book chapters, and nearly 50 books in print or preparation. His research on religion, health and ethical issues in medicine has been featured on dozens of national and international TV news programs (including ABC's World News Tonight, The Today Show, Good Morning America. Dr. Oz Show, and NBC Nightly News), over a hundred national or international radio programs, and hundreds of newspapers and magazines (including Reader's Digest, Parade Magazine, Newsweek, Time, and Guidepost). Dr. Koenig has given testimony before the U.S. Senate (1998) and U.S. House of Representatives (2008) concerning the benefits of religion and spirituality on public health, and travels widely to give seminars and workshops on this topic. He is the recipient of the 2012 Oskar Pfister Award from the American Psychiatric Association.

Printed in Great Britain
by Amazon

55849808R00061